The Meditations of
Elton Trueblood

The Meditations of
ELTON
TRUEBLOOD

Edited by Stephen R. Sebert
and W. Gordon Ross

1817

HARPER & ROW, PUBLISHERS
New York, Evanston, San Francisco, London

FIRST EDITION

Designed by Eve Callahan

Library of Congress Cataloging in Publication Data

Trueblood, David Elton, 1900-
   The meditations of Elton Trueblood.
    1. Meditations. 2. Yokefellow Movement. I. Title.
BV4832.2.T78 1975   242   75-9340
ISBN 0-06-068671-5

75 76 77 78 79 80 10 9 8 7 6 5 4 3 2 1

LtP

Contents

Acknowledgments

The gathering and assembling of the materials for this book has been the work of many Yokefellows. We want especially to recognize the contribution of Mary Perdue in typing the parts of the manuscript written by Stephen R. Sebert, also the encouragement she has been in all phases of the book's development. The important background, dates, and detail on the Yokefellow Movement came from the records of Yokefellows International. Robert Pitman, their executive secretary, has collected these records and graciously made them available to us.

The directors of the Yokefellow centers and ministries cooperated speedily in sending needed information. In recognition of their contribution and the nature of this book all the royalties from this book will go to the ministry of Yokefellows at Shakertown, Kentucky.

STEPHEN R. SEBERT
W. GORDON ROSS

Preface

We are calling this collection a garnering of wisdom, conviction, and inspiration of Elton Trueblood. He did not know back in 1951 when preparing *The Life We Prize* for publication that he was making a statement that could be used on such an occasion as this to celebrate what he was then doing and would continue to do for many more years. Consider the following sentences from that book: "What we seek, as we face the task of living with other people, is some guiding principle which may help to bring order out of our daily confusion. This has been sought for centuries by some of the best minds which our race has known and these have left us a *garnered wisdom*" (italics supplied).

These meditations, the final selection and editing of which were the work of W. Gordon Ross, number one hundred and are grouped into three divisions. The first gives expression to the theme of fellowship, of human beings in various groupings, including the family. The second gives attention to the idea of God. The third highlights the theme of our life in, and our involvement with, the world, with its tragedies and triumphs, its vices and victories, its threats and opportunities. The meditations are accompanied by Scriptural references, with the

hope they may take readers into further recognition of the
Bible as a resource for moral and spiritual living.

Letters at the end of each quotation indicate the book from
which the selection is taken. (See list on copyright page.) It
has hardly been feasible to make use of all of Trueblood's
works for present space limitations.

The American bicentennial and the occasion of Elton Trueblood's seventy-fifth birthday on December 12 provide ample
incentives to review his writings. Add the continuing collapse
of Western civilization and the incentive becomes a demand
to reexamine the methods used by the church to revitalize our
culture. One of these methods is renewal of which Trueblood
is a major proponent.

As you read this book remember the contexts of his writings. The church responded to the crisis of our civilization by
proposing three different methods of recovery: revival, revolution, or renewal. These methods are not necessarily exclu-
sive of one another but they are distinct.

The decade of the fifties saw the rise of revivalism to
national prominence. The attempt at revival built and filled
many buildings. But the fruits of revival were short-lived or at
least proved inadequate to revive our cities. Our cities are the
heart of our civilization.

The sixties became the decade for revolution. The cry for
revolt brought some change and aided the attempt at The Great
Society. Revolution has changed the face of the city but failed
to call her to become "The City of God." The cry for revolution
scared many persons but it produced more fear than hope.
"White flight" is a clear example of the result of fear.

The third alternative method espoused by the church became
a movement for renewal. This movement still has many eclec-
tic tendencies. In order for it to become a genuine instrument
of renewal its identity and purpose needs more focus. In the
meditations of Trueblood are found some of the Biblical, his-

torical, and philosophical perspectives needed to focus renewal. Renewal as a movement can bring the needed hope, power, and vision to our cities.

The purpose of this book, in addition to providing a collection of meditations, is to call for a fuller examination of a man, his message, and the movement for renewal.

S.R.S.
W.G.R.

The Meditations of Elton Trueblood

edited by W. Gordon Ross

I
People in Groups
1–34

1

All evils, He (Christ) thus taught, have internal origins. The deepest sins are spiritual rather than physical. (HC 17)

Christ had to wage a battle because the things for which He stood were intrinsically threatening to those in power, either politically or religiously. The fierceness of the struggle made choice necessary and with choice came inevitable division among men. The people who wanted to smooth things over and to be friends with everybody, thus avoiding all tension, were simply naïve, for life is not ordered that way. Herein lies the tremendous import of Christ's words, "Do not think that I have come to bring peace on earth; I have not come to bring peace, but a sword" (Matt. 10:34 RSV). (HC 68)

He (Christ) saw, at the start, that the fundamental dangers were not single, but were dual or even multiple. It is always true, so far as can be seen, that any possible alternative to a particular error *may* be another error. If the only alternative to an error were the truth, life would be simple, but that is precisely what life never is. Therefore, since the possibilities of evil are plural, we must beware of moving from one of these to another. There is no advantage in escaping from the fire into the frying pan. (HC 71)

There is no man more vulnerable and therefore more ridiculous than one who claims to be perfect. Human perfection is a worthwhile goal, providing we are realistic enough to know that we do not attain it. But the man who claims attainment is wide open to attack. (HC 79)

Few features of official religion, of any particular faith, are more open to ridicule than is ostentation. The Christian faith, which began with an emphasis upon simplicity and humility, as vividly illustrated by the acted parable of the washing of the disciples' feet, has succumbed, in various generations, to the temptation to grandeur. Christ saw it coming and gave advance warning, though the warning has been seldom heeded. (HC 84)

Read: Zechariah 4:1–6; Ephesians 6:10–20

2

When we say that the most urgent problem of our time is the spiritual problem we are opposing directly the popular opinion. *Most people do not believe it.* It is curious to note the way in which our world calamity has destroyed some of our comfortable delusions, but not others. Thus we have been pretty well emancipated from the dogma of automatic progress and even from faith in the goodness of man. . . . But we have not been equally emancipated from the belief that economic and technical reconstruction are enough. We suppose, quite naïvely, that the problem of spiritual reconstruction will take care of itself or that it can be left to the experts as a departmental matter. (PMM 17)

One of the most disturbing of the parables of Jesus is the parable of the empty house (Matthew 12:43–45). The house, we are told, was emptied of the unclean spirit that had occupied it and was swept and garnished. *But it could not remain empty.* Not only did the original evil spirit return, but seven other devils, worse than the first, accompanied him. We have already seen this development in parts of our culture, and we shall see it in other parts unless we follow a more intelligent course of action. The empty condition, spiritually, is a condition of the greatest danger.

The danger of emptiness is seen vividly in the desire for unity and community. (PMM 51)

Ephesians 2:19   Thus you are strangers and foreigners no longer, you share the membership of the saints, you belong to God's own household. . . . (Moffatt)
I Corinthians 3:9   We work together in God's service; you are God's field to be planted, God's house to be built. (Moffatt)

3

The task, then, is still before us—the task of making a decent world in our modern technical age, *after* the elimination of such open enemies of Christian civilization as Hitler and his kind. *We have argued that this cannot be accomplished without ethical convictions, that the ethical convictions cannot be made to prevail if separated from their religious roots, and that the religious roots cannot be nourished apart from the organized church or something like it.* If this reasoning is sound, we are carried forward to a final question concerning the nature of the organized movements without which civilization as we know it will perish. We need to be both precise and concrete in our proposals. (PMM 91–92)

The idea that salvation, both for individuals and society, comes through the work of living fellowships is as old as Christianity and older. We have said that it is incumbent upon the children of light to borrow the wisdom of the children of this world but the borrowing was the other way around, inasmuch as the technic which Hitler so carefully describes is essentially the technic of the first Christian victory. John the Baptist was a voice crying in the wilderness, but Jesus was not, because he depended on the way in which twelve men were bound together. The fellowship of the Nazi party members is a kind of parody of the *Koinonia*. (PMM 99–100)

Deuteronomy 30:19 f. . . . here and now I call heaven and earth to witness against you that I have put life and death before you, the blessing and the curse: choose life, then, that you and your children may live, by loving the Eternal your God, obeying his voice, and holding fast to him, for that means life to you and length of days. . . . (Moffatt)

4

Worship, at its best, is a group experience. The individual on the lonely hillside may know the real presence of God, but there he is only one, and there are many to assert that, when they are with a company, each individual is more than himself. If there is any reality in the group idea, if there is any experience in which men become knit together into an organic whole and cease to be independent units like marbles in a bag, we should expect to find this deeper unity in worship. The very faces of the other persons present can help us; they can fill us with a new sense of the similarity of our problems and the common elements of our human nature. That is why an ordinary service of worship is so different from the experience of sitting alone at home listening to a sermon over the radio. As we listen to the radio we are not *participators*, but in every real service of worship each person contributes to the total mood, by the very expression on his face if in no other way. It is not uncommon for thoughts and hopes to be generated in an hour of group worship that are larger than, and different from, the combined thoughts and hopes of the various individuals on entering the building. When this happens worship is really *creative*. (ESR 82–83)

If we begin to see how worship may be a creative group enterprise we soon realize that every effort at worship is an exciting venture. Such worship may have an order of service, but it certainly will not be a recital of what has already been learned. It is not like the playing of a phonograph record. If each person, including the minister, were to go to the service full of expectancy and wonder, realizing that a creative venture was about to be undertaken in which the total result was quite unpredictable, then we would be justified in talking about the worship which is "in spirit and in truth." (ESR 83)

Psalm 44:1   O God, we have heard with our ears, our fathers have told us the tale, of thy doings in ancient years. . . . (Moffatt)
Read: Psalm 78:2–8

5

The search for new light is entered into by those who attempt to be members one of another and who seek light in the spirit of reverence. It should be understood that the word "group" is here used in a special sense. By a group is meant a fairly small company of persons already having enough in common to start thinking and seeking together without embarrassment. A large company, of several hundred or more, cannot be expected to carry on group thought or seek group guidance. Most of us have little circles of which we are integral parts and to which we can submit our deepest decisions. In the general experience of the race, group life has been as real as individual life, but we have often failed to take advantage of the fact. (ESR 124)

Group life becomes for many a reality in the experience of worship, but if we are to accept the notion of a worship that covers all existence, we may expect the same kind of group experience in common decisions. What should the individual do if the guidance of the group differs from his own? It would be dangerous to say that he should always give up his own convictions, for history has shown that the lone individual is sometimes right. The individual should ask the group to help him with his problem and should try to become part of the group as the matter is considered. He may find that he is still convinced of what is truth for him, though the group does not agree, and then he must go forward according to the light he sees, but always in great humility. (ESR 125)

Read: Galatians 6:1–8

6

One of the best examples of how the individual may be conscious of his group life and yet resolute in his own path is seen in the decision of John Woolman to go to England on a religious visit. Before he went he presented his "concern" to his fellows at home and they agreed that it was right for him to go. Several thought he should go as comfortably as possible, but his mind was not easy in the cabin with its superfluity of decorations, so, in much discomfort, he went in the steerage. When he arrived in England the Londoners were somewhat condescending to the rural-looking New Jersey tailor and it was the considered judgment of the group to which he went that he should return home without delivering his message. Woolman was much saddened by this decision, and told his religious guests that he would not be a burden to them since he knew a trade, but he did not feel free to return home. In other words, Woolman acquiesced in the decision of the group in one way and yet not in another. He differed from the group almost in fear and yet he could not be untrue to the truth as he saw it. His individualism was severely limited and he did not disregard the rights of others. It is almost needless to say that Woolman's mixture of submissiveness and strength of character was so appealing that the whole group was mellowed and asked him to go forward at once with his message. (ESR 125–126)

James 5:11   See, we call the steadfast happy; you have heard of the steadfastness of Job, and you have seen the end of the Lord with him, seen that the Lord is very compassionate and (full of pity). (Moffatt)

7

If we ask how this most remarkable of the miracles of history (early Christianity) was performed, we are amazed at the simplicity of the method. The world needed a saving faith and the formula was that such a faith comes by a particular kind of fellowship. Jesus was deeply concerned for the continuation of his redemptive work after the close of his earthly existence, and his chosen method was *the formation of a redemptive society*. He did not form an army, establish a headquarters, or even write a book. All he did was to collect a few unpromising men, inspire them with the sense of his vocation and theirs, and build their lives into an intensive fellowship of affection, worship and work. ... (AF 29)

One of the truly shocking passages of the Gospel is that in which Jesus indicates that there is absolutely no substitute for the tiny redemptive society. If this fails, he suggests, all is failure; there is no other way. The Sermon on the Mount is largely directed to making the little band understand this momentous fact, and to prepare for the consequent burden by adequate discipline. Here the key passage is the metaphor of salt. He told the little bedraggled fellowship that they were actually the salt of the earth and that, if this salt should fail, there would be no adequate preservative at all. . . . (AF 29–30)

II Timothy 1:14   Keep the great securities of your faith intact, by aid of the holy Spirit that dwells within us. (Moffatt)

Zechariah 8:16   Fear not! This is what you must do: let every man tell the truth, in dealing with his neighbour, let your decisions in court be true and for the common good. . . . (Moffatt)

8

That the unqualified words of the Sermon on the Mount were addressed to a small group is part of our amazement, especially when we know how weak and fallible its members were. The group at that time included Judas, who turned out to be a traitor, Peter, who showed himself a coward, and the sons of Zebedee, who were crudely ambitious of personal advancement. Sometimes we picture the Sermon on the Mount, which is the charter of the redemptive society, as being given to a great crowd, but the New Testament distinctly says otherwise. "And seeing the multitudes, he went up into a mountain; and when he was set, his disciples came unto him: and he opened his mouth, and taught them, saying. . . . Ye are the salt of the earth" (AV). (AF 30)

The idea of a redemptive fellowship, so amazingly central to Christianity, involves an entire philosophy of civilization. How is civilization changed? It is changed, early Christianity answers, by the creation of fellowships which eventually become infectious in the entire cultural order. We are surprised to see how little the early Christians dealt with current political and economic problems, if we may judge by the extant literature of the period. They did not even attack slavery, iniquitous as it must have been. They just went on building the kind of fellowship which was bound, eventually, to destroy slavery. All this seems alien to our modern mentality, but it may involve divine wisdom. In any case, we should not be too proud to try, for we are not doing so well on our present line of endeavor. It helps our modesty to realize that these ancient men were accused of turning the world upside down, whereas no one would accuse us of anything similar. Instead of turning the world upside down, we feel helpless as we watch the rising spiral of inflationary prices, observe with some foreboding the actions of little men in Washington and go to the races. (AF 31–32)

Isaiah 59:1–2   The Eternal's hand is not too short to save, the Eternal's ear is not too dull to hear! It is your own iniquities that interfere between your God and you; your sins have made him veil his face from you, until he will not listen. (Moffatt)

9

The sense of membership in a redemptive society would dignify individual lives in that it would give meaning to history, along with a sense of human solidarity, since membership involves men in a longitudinal, as well as a latitudinal, fellowship. There has been an enduring and continuous community, beginning with a suppressed people who were preserved through all kinds of danger for the sake of a divine purpose which was destined to include all humanity. The heroes and prophets of this tradition may be spiritual ancestors of us all regardless of our biological inheritance. . . . Early Christians were thrilled as they thought of themselves as part of (an) emerging divine purpose. They had a link with eternity because in their fellowship they were partners in the creative love that made the world. (AF 32)

It is perfectly clear that the same method could be effective again, if we could have the simplicity to try it. Men who are partners in the redemptive task of God Himself have all the dignity of personal life that is required to lift them out of mediocrity, but their glorification does not come at the expense of others or by means of antagonism. It was a cardinal point in the redemptive fellowships which changed the ancient world that all human barriers must be transcended. There is no longer Jew or Gentile, no longer bond or free. The work is grounded in history, quite as truly as is the work of the convinced Nazi . . . but it involves no struggle against other races or other classes. . . . Their creed is summarized by the conviction that "In all things, God works for good *with* them who love Him." (AF 33)

Ephesians 2:14   For he is our *peace*, he who has made both of us a unity and destroyed the barrier which kept us apart. . . . (Moffatt)

10

We now have a clue which may guide us in the recovery of a sense of meaning in our lives. We find this clue in the concept of faith through a special kind of fellowship. It is something which was once proposed, once tried and once found to succeed. That it succeeded so abundantly is our chief basis of hope, because there is reason to believe that *what has been can again be.* In our dire extremity, marked especially by a sense of futility, we are justified in turning with hope to the most striking example of spiritual revival which the history of the world can show. (AF 36)

In turning to this example we need to remind ourselves again that that with which we are dealing is sober history. The redemptive effect of the little Christian community on the ancient civilized world is no fairy story. It is not a fantastic tale produced by an imaginative writer; it is not a philosophy of civilization which some thinker constructed in the privacy of his study; *it occurred.* Conscious of a divine destiny and filled with love of the brethren, the little groups once established at Philippi, Corinth, and Ephesus finally altered the structure and tone of ancient culture. (AF 36–37)

What we require is the same courage in trying to see what a church might be. Fortunately we know something about the original reaction; amazing things might occur to us if we could view it afresh. We should not then despise our fathers or our fathers' fathers but should seek to get as close as possible to the reality of which their particular societies were distant reflections. Of course neither we nor the chemists can succeed wholly in going behind accepted procedures, but it is nevertheless worth trying. *Columbus did not succeed in reaching China, but he found America.* (AF 48)

Proverbs 9:9   Instruct a man of sense, and he will gain more sense; teach a good man, and he will learn the more. (Moffatt)

Proverbs 10:11, 13   The talk of good men is a life-giving fountain: the talk of bad men overflows with harm. . . . Good sense is on the lips of the intelligent, but folly lies in the talk of senseless men. (Moffatt)

11

Living in a time which provides us with so much relevant contemporary experience, as well as the experience of former generations, we should be able to employ a disciplined imagination to good advantage in determining what the essential features of a truly redemptive society may be. We live in what seems to be a time of unusual ferment and it is good to be a part of this intellectual agitation. (AF 53)

Almost any business in the world can be undertaken redemptively, partly because each is concerned with persons and there are always numerous personal contacts in any business. What we have a right to expect now is the emergence of creative thinking about the application of lay religion to areas of common life. This is our most important twentieth-century frontier. Some people are already giving their thoughts to the development of this frontier and new ideas are appearing in heartening numbers. (SoH 95)

The history of Christianity has been that of the emergence of truly redemptive fellowships, the Order of the Salt, and their eventual decay, as religion has become a dull and almost meaningless affair or the professional concern of a priestly group. But the salt has never lost its savor so badly that renewal was impossible.... (SoH 108)

I Peter 3:8–10   Lastly, you must all be united, you must have sympathy, brotherly love, compassion, and humility, never paying back evil for evil, never reviling when you are reviled, but on the contrary blessing. For this is your vocation, to bless and to inherit blessing; he who would love Life and enjoy good days, let him keep his tongue from evil and his lips from speaking guile.... (Moffatt)

12

One good way to make the meaning of this deeper fellowship clear is to contrast it with the once popular discussion group. Once the discussion group seemed a great discovery and it became the central feature of student religious gatherings. It seemed wonderful because it was so much better than the mere passive listening to lectures. But we realize today that there is something as far beyond the discussion group as it was beyond the lecture. This new emphasis is not upon argument *about* God, but obedience *to* God. We realize that the discussion group may not be really religious in essence, even if it is devoted to religious questions, and may be actually *sacrilegious.* Discussion is a valuable human experience, but it is the beginning rather than the end, and it does not really belong to the same universe of discourse as does personal dedication. . . . *In so far as we have really gone forward in creative Christian minorities in the midst of the world civil war, that advancement may be conveniently symbolized by the movement from discussion to commitment.* . . . (SoH 112)

The committed groups, whose fellowship differs in kind from the conviviality of the fraternities and clubs, find that they are driven, in nearly all instances, to the acceptance of voluntary discipline. The majority may still be satisfied with the now outmoded philosophy of self-expression, but the creative minorities have usually discovered the power which discipline releases and the freedom which it makes possible. It is easy for me to see that the disciplined pianist is far more free in his movements that I am; he is free to put his fingers on the right keys at the right time and I am not. The new movement we are noting as an evidence of hope in a century of storm accepts this conclusion, not only for art and music, but likewise for the life of the spirit. (SoH 113)

I Timothy 1:4b–5   . . . such studies bear upon speculations rather than on the divine order which belongs to faith. Whereas the aim of the Christian discipline is the love that springs from a pure heart, from a good conscience, and from a sincere faith. (Moffatt)

13

Friends soon saw that the final justification of the fellowship was the creative way in which it led people into the service of their fellow men. A concern arises when the deep experience of the knowledge of God as revealed by Christ, and especially that knowledge which emerges in the minds of a genuine fellowship, leads those thus shaken to perform deeds of mercy to their neighbors wherever found. Thus the concern accomplishes the marriage of the inner and the outer; it joins, in miraculous fashion, the roots and the fruits of religion. (AF 99)

When only the roots are emphasized, we have a situation in which people luxuriate in their own religious emotions, developing their inner experiences for their own sake. It is easy for religion to stop here, but when it does, we have little more than spiritual sensuality. It is fundamentally self-centered. Where, on the other hand, only the fruits are emphasized, we have mere creaturely activity, the kind of worldly philanthropy which eventually is little more than professional social service. Friends, in their long history, have often made both of these mistakes, but the major tradition has been the avoidance of both by keeping the connection close. Worship of God is one thing and service of mankind is another, but the first is dishonest unless it eventuates in the latter and the latter is superficial unless it springs from the former. A realization of this had led many Friends to think of John Woolman as their best exemplar. (AF 99)

Psalm 71:16   I will recite the great deeds of the Lord, and praise thy faithful aid—and only thine. (Moffatt)

Isaiah 65:11   But ye who have forsaken the Eternal, ye who ignore his sacred hill, spreading tables to Good Luck, pouring libations to Fate, I make the sword your fate. . . . (Moffatt)

14

As we analyze the experiences of the faithful and courageous minorities we find that there is one factor which all
have in common, *the acceptance of discipline.* The Orthodox
Jews have the discipline of the refusal to eat pork, of the
separate Sabbath, and of the specially donned clothing during
the prayer. All this makes them a people apart, sometimes
persecuted and despised, but the discipline, however trivial it
may seem, is a source of strength. The faithful Roman Catho-
lic has the discipline of confession, of early Mass, of the Friday
fast. This last may be largely fictitious, since fish is regularly
substituted for meat, but the very reminder is helpful to many.
In any case, it is beneficent to have the ordinary Western rule
of self-indulgence and doing what you please limited at even
a few points. The Mormon has the discipline of the renuncia-
tion of alcohol, coffee, tea, and tobacco, along with the far
more revolutionary practice of giving one or two years in missionary labor at his own expense. The Adventist has the discipline of the Saturday rest and worship, often at the expense of
ridicule, and he has the still more difficult discipline of giving
rigidly one-tenth of his net income to the spread of the gospel.
The Intervarsity Christian Fellowship often seems woefully out
of date in its theology, sometimes being frankly fundamen-
talist, but it now flourishes on several hundred campuses,
appealing to students and instructors of high intelligence largely
because it is definite in its requirements, especially in regard to
regular daily prayer. (AF 84–85)

Read: Proverbs 1:7–27

15

Here, then, is our clue, if we wish to regain lost ground in the spiritual life. We should try to have the *right* discipline, but the primary requirement is that we have *a* discipline. Almost any rule is better than none. "There is not that thing in the world," wrote Milton, "of more grave and urgent importance throughout the whole life of man, than is discipline" (*The Reason for Church Government*, chap. i). A few years ago it seemed to us that these words of the seventeenth century were an overstatement, but now we are not so sure that we were right. In any case, here is a concrete starting point for any who have become conscious of the futility and flabbiness of our modern life and wish to do something positive about it. (AF 88)

The evidence is really overwhelming. *Powerful groups, for whatever ends, are disciplined groups, whereas libertarian movements end in futility.* This is the clear lesson of history, and it is not likely that our generation will provide an exception to the rule. The person who gets up to attend early Mass is more likely to spread his faith than is the person who, with exquisite self-indulgence, reads the Sunday paper all morning. The man who reads Scripture or prayers each day is more likely to be a revolutionary force in our civilization than is his neighbor whose reading, whether at home or on the train, is largely confined to that amazing symbol of our contemporary culture, the *comic book*. (AF 91–92)

Read: Proverbs 15:28–32

16

The Quaker discipline, which was extremely strict for about two hundred years, is one of the best known in the modern world. Everyone is acquainted with the pictures of men in plain coat and hat, and everyone has at least heard of the plain language of "thee" and "thou," even though these forms have been given up, for the most part, for more than a generation. Was the strict Quaker discipline of an earlier day a mistake or not? It is hard to know. It is easy to see why the strictness kept a man like Walt Whitman from joining the fellowship even though he was deeply drawn to it on other grounds, and we can all have some sympathy with Dr. Johnson when he said that a man who could not get into heaven in a green coat would not get there sooner in a gray one. But, having recognized these difficulties, we must also admit that the older Quaker discipline was a source of enormous moral strength. (The same conclusion applies to Brethren, Mennonites, and all "plain people.") It was like high straight banks, which make a stream run swiftly instead of spreading into swamps. In the lives of John Woolman, Elizabeth Fry, John Greenleaf Whittier, and many more the disciplined simplicity of speech, clothing, and manner of life released energy for social concern. We have now given it up, but what have we put in its place? (AF 90–91)

Read: Matthew 5:33–37

17

The following *minimum discipline* is suggested, not as a finished product or as in any way ideal, but as a possible starting point for any group of concerned people, anywhere, who are tired of waiting and propose now to *begin*. Each point may be elaborated and probably some new points should be added. Certainly individuals will find it wise to add those points especially relevant to their particular situations, needs, and temptations. The points now tentatively suggested are: 1. Worship.

2. Solitude. 3. Silence. 4. Humanity. 5. Austerity. (AF 100–102)

The best prayer is seldom a hit-and-miss matter, but grows by the glad acceptance of discipline, which, far from being its antithesis, is the price of real freedom. Herein lies the deep wisdom of the Yoke passage (Matthew 11:29, 30). Just as all empty freedom inevitably turns into bondage, so the acceptance of Christ's yoke sets men free. It does not eliminate burdens, but because the yoke fits, the burdens actually seem light. In Christ's teaching the practice of devotion is the first step of a series in which freedom is the final consequence. "If you continue in my word, you are truly my disciples, and you will know the truth, and the truth will make you free" (John 8:31, 32 RSV). (PS 103)

Matthew 11:27–30   All has been handed over to me by my Father: and no one knows the Son except the Father—nor does anyone know the Father except the Son, and he to whom the Son chooses to reveal him. Come to me, all ye labouring and burdened, and I will refresh you. Take my yoke upon you and learn from me, for I am gentle and humble in heart, and you will find your souls refreshed; my yoke is kindly and my burden light. (Moffatt)

18

It may be easier to be a saint without being surrounded by the persistent claims of little children, but the easier sainthood is of much less value. What we seek is not merely a fellowship of *individuals*, but a fellowship of *families*. It must be kept close to common life, with all of its heavy responsibilities and attendant opportunities. The fellowship must be *in* the world though not *of* it; it is not that of the monastery, but that of the market place and ordinary professions. The glorification of common life is a higher ideal than is the cultivation of the separated

community, no matter how peaceful the lives of its inmates
may be. (AF 120–121)

Important as daily work may be, in the experience of the
ordinary human being, the life of his family is far more important. His pride and his ambition may be involved in his professional advancement, but far more than pride and ambition
are involved in his relationship to his *home*. Most people, when
they earn money, need the money not as individuals, but as
breadwinners for several others, including the young and helpless. Accordingly, all the deeper emotions are involved in the
effort to support and maintain family life. (YOV 80)

Read: Ephesians 3:14–19

19

There is a more continuous opportunity for an effective
Christian ministry in the home than anywhere else in the
world. What goes on in churches is highly important, but it is
always in some degree abstract, in that most of what is said to
one another is out of its immediate practical context. We talk,
in church, about moral values, but we talk of them in separation from the situations in which most problems arise. In a
home, however, when parents instruct their children or engage
in family conferences and worship, the ministry of word and
deed is in the closest contact with the practical problems. The
situations of selfishness and of lack of concern for others are
handled directly and *in context*. Accordingly such ministry,
even though the congregation is tiny, is in close touch with
reality. (YOV 81)

No matter how much a man may be concerned with his work
in the world, he cannot normally *care* about it as much as he
cares about his family. This is because we have, in the life of
the family, a bigger stake than most of us can ever have in our

employment. We can change business associates, if we need to, and we can leave a poor job for a better one, but we cannot change *sons*. If we lose the struggle in our occupational interests, we can try again, but if we lose with our children our loss is terribly and frighteningly *final*. A man who cares more for his work than he cares for his family is generally accounted abnormal or perverse and justifiably so. He is one who has not succeeded in getting his values straight; he fails to recognize what the true priorities are. (YOV 82)

Read: Titus 2:1–8

20

We may truly say that just as the lay ministry finds a fuller expression in ordinary daily work than it does in a church, so it finds a fuller expression in the family than in employment, and perhaps more in the family than anywhere else in our world. If our religion does not lift the level of our family life it is not likely to be sincere or really effective at any other point. What occurs at the altar is insignificant unless what occurs there is supported by what occurs in the kitchen. The sermons by which Christian men and women may be rightly judged are the silent sermons of cooperative affection. (YOV 82)

The family is the only institution in our world where the Kingdom of God can actually begin. This is not to paint a rosy or sentimental picture of what family life actually is. Of course, there are tensions and sometimes the strain seems so unbearable that the whole experiment ends in failure. Husbands and wives sometimes turn against each other with vindictive hatred and the same is true of parents and children, but, in an enormous number of cases, the presence of strain does not exclude a continuing and redemptive love. There are many families in which the members can truly report that, though life has been far from easy, never once has there been a real break in affection and never once has there been a struggle for power, such as most societies outside the home, including religious ones, so often exhibit. We know that homes are places where it is possible for love to be supreme and we do not know any others. (YOV 94–95)

Read: Psalm 103:1–13

21

We do not claim to have any easy answers to problems (of mothers earning or needing to earn, for example), but we are very sure of two things. First, those of us who do not face this economic and social problem must be very tender toward those who do, and, second, we must understand clearly the human harm which comes as the family withers away at important levels in our society. Only as we understand the loss will we have the incentive adequate to make us use our imagination to reverse the process of decay. (RFL 26–27)

The institution of the family is such an enormous success in the sense that it endures through change, that we may be sure of its continuation in some form. But the danger is that it may continue in some withered form rather than in full health. Because there are several different forms which family life can take, we must use intelligence to choose among them and guide our course accordingly. (RFL 38)

If the hard-pressed men and women in the little homes, who are faced with difficulties every day, can be made to feel that they, in maintaining families, are in a crucial position, doing that which the world sorely needs and without which the world will go to pieces, they may be enabled to face their tasks with a wholly new spirit. It is the responsibility of every reader of this book to feel this sense of vocation in trying to make his own home into a place where the Christian revolution begins, and to spread this idea to as many others as possible. (RFL 127)

Read: Luke 10:38–42

22

Personal happiness must never become our chief end or goal. The purpose is not to be happy, but to perpetuate what is best for human life. Of course happiness usually comes in such a procedure, but it comes as a by-product. Emerson says wisely that the beauty of the sunrise or sunset is greatest when it comes as a surprise by the way. It is one lesson of the history of philosophical thought that the only way to *get* happiness is to *forget* it. Just as our popular philosophy is ambiguous about happiness it is likewise ambiguous about self-expression. Just what do we mean by it? *Which* side of ourselves do we propose to express? The idea of self-expression does not really help us, since the beastly side can be expressed just as the potential nobility can be expressed. Anyone who expressed all his thoughts and obeyed all his impulses would surely reveal himself as an utter fool. (RFL 49)

One of the greatest blessings which can come to any normal child is the existence of two parents. There are, of course, numerous persons who grow to splendid maturity without this advantage, but they are forced to overcome a serious handicap in the process. The mother and the father are both helpful to the child and to the home as a whole, partly because they are different, psychologically as well as physically. The importance of the father in the home does not rest upon the absurd belief that men and women ought to play the same role, but rather on the recognition that their roles are different, complementary, and equally necessary. (RFL 88)

Read: Matthew 18:1–6

23

It is a sobering experience to see the bitterness of young people, sometimes of college age, who feel that they have been cheated in that their parents have never given them adequate time. This is particularly true when both parents have lived public lives and the children have been given a steady diet of boarding school in the winter, with camp in the summer, but no real home life. The fact that such people often have had plenty of money is no substitute for what is so sorely missed. It is in such ways that parents frequently pay a higher personal price for worldly success than they at first realize or than the world knows. The children of parents in modest circumstances are, for these reasons, usually more fortunate. (RFL 91)

The wise parent will be very attentive to see what it is that children desire. One of the strongest of the child's desires is to be *proud* of his parents. He wants this more than he wants money and even more than he wants time. He wants to know that others admire the ones he loves. Therefore the father who makes a public disgrace of his life or appears in a ridiculous light before his child's friends is making a deep wound. It is right that a parent should ask frequently, in regard to some proposed course of action, "Will this make my child proud of me or ashamed of me?" This is a point very easy for mothers to forget, but they do so at great peril. The mother who neglects her own appearance, in order to give a better costume to her daughter, is undoubtedly doing so out of affection, but the affection is usually misguided, because what the daughter wants is that her mother should be admired by the daughter's contemporaries. (RFL 93)

Read: I Samuel 2:1–10; Luke 1:46–55

24

After all the familiar criticisms have been leveled at the existent churches, the fact remains that periods of crisis often reveal real differences between the Church and the surrounding world. The Church is divided, as other organizations, such as parties and clubs, are divided, but with the enormous difference that millions of church members consider their division a scandal and are trying mightily to do something about it, whereas divisiveness outside seems perfectly normal. The Church often reflects the ordinary standards of the world, but in many heartening cases it represents a different and far more humane standard.

A striking example of this was provided during World War II, when American citizens were forcibly removed from their homes in Pacific coast states because they were of Japanese ancestry. All are now enabled to know how exceedingly unjust and how unnecessary this action was, inasmuch as the Congressional inquiry has failed to find a single authenticated case of sabotage by these people. Many suffered severe economic loss, disruption of careers and of schooling, in addition to the psychological harm of being treated as third-class citizens. A large proportion of our population knows this now, but the point is that those who knew it at the time, and had the courage to say so, were people whose idealism had been mediated to them through the fellowship which began long ago in the mind of Christ. A representative body of Japanese-Americans has recently reported, to their amazement, that all the people who helped them in relocation or education or care of property were acting from definite Christian inspiration. *The patriotic societies did not help them, but the Christian societies did.* Such an example is good to remember when criticism is most sweeping and vicious. (AF 38–39)

Read: Matthew 25:40–46

25

An argument has been presented for volunteer Christian work, both on the part of the older persons who are free to give full time to the church and on the part of those who, because they are regularly employed, can give away only a margin of their time. We are making a serious mistake, however, if, in stressing this volunteer work, we seem to suggest that work is not Christian work unless it is work for the churches. Actually the witness made in regular employment may be far more significant and productive than any service rendered in free time. It is a gross error to suppose that the Christian cause goes forward solely or chiefly on week ends. What happens on the regular week days may be far more important, so far as the Christian faith is concerned, than what happens on Sundays. A minority ought to leave their secular employment in order to engage in full-time work, for the promotion of the gospel, but this is not true of most. Most men ought to stay where they are and to make their Christian witness *in* ordinary work rather than beyond it. A deeply concerned banker may be sorely tempted to leave his bank in order to give his full time to some volunteer service, but deeper reflection may show him that this would be a mistake. The investment of funds, especially for great charities, may be a task which it would be wrong for such a man to escape. (YOV, 57–58)

One of the heartening developments of our time has been the

growing awareness, on the part of those touched by the Christian gospel, of the meaning of vocation. The idea is that God can call us to many kinds of activity and that secular work well done is a holy enterprise. (YOV 58)

Read: Matthew 10:5–8

26

In spite of all the variations of Christian belief, there has normally been, and there is now, a central stream of thought. What we denote as basic Christianity is that which exists at the center of the Christian spectrum. Far from being sectarian, it is represented in nearly all denominations. This central stream is both rational and evangelical. The essential feature is commitment to Jesus Christ, who told His followers to love God with all their minds (Mark 12:30). (PS 33)

While there are many current evidences of decay, there is also a saving remnant, especially among those of the silent center. In spite of the much-publicized erosion of faith, large segments of our people accept Christ as the surest reality of their lives; they truly love God, and they engage in service to their fellow men which is motivated by this love. The strange fact, however, is that the vast majority of contemporary Christians have no adequate voice, because they have so few spokesmen to whom the intellectual world is willing to listen. The tendency is to give major attention, and the headline, to faddists. We must develop spokesmen who are able to articulate the faith of the great body of Christians who, though they seldom speak up, are tremendously important. (PS 34)

Read: Matthew 6:6–8; 22:35–40

27

The word "vocation" has been debased in the modern world by being made synonymous with "occupation," but it is one of the gains of our time that the old word is beginning to regain its original meaning of "calling." "Behold your calling, brethren," is the old text which is now achieving new significance. On the purely secular basis the term "vocation" is practically meaningless, since, unless God really is, there is no one to do the calling, but, on the Christian basis, it is a reasonable word. It still refers, in many cases, to occupation, but the conception is that each occupation can and must be conceived as a *ministry*. (YOV 63)

The exciting idea behind the New Testament use of "calling" is that ours is God's world, in all its parts. The way in which we grow potatoes is as much a matter of God's will as is the way in which we pray or sing. Of all precious elements in God's world, men and women are most precious, because they share something of the divine life, particularly in the capacity to be creative. Toil then becomes holy, because it is by toil that men can prove themselves creatures made in God's image. If God is the Worker, then men and women, in order to fulfill their potentialities, must be workers, too. They are sharing in creation when they develop a farm, paint a picture, build a home, or polish a floor. (YOV 63–64)

II Timothy 2:14, 15   Remind men of this: adjure them before the Lord not to bandy arguments—no good comes out of that, it only means the undoing of your audience. Do your utmost to let God see that you at least are a sound workman, with no need to be ashamed of the way you handle the word of the Truth. (Moffatt)

28

The shame of many a supposed home today is that it is
largely a place where people sleep part of the night, but not
really a scene of uniting experiences of all members, older and
younger. Common meals become more and more infrequent
while unhurried family conferences are out of the question. It
is futile to talk to people about grace at meals if they do not
even have the meals. A couple who have to do all the house-
work late at night, after tiring and nervously demanding hours
in the business of the day, are not prepared for family worship
or even family affection. Countless supposed homes become
places of bickering and of constant bitterness when the members do finally assemble. What could be the most wonderful of
human associations thus becomes one of the worst. (YOV 85)

Important as the economic factors may be in the decay of
family life, they are not the most basic ones. Far more basic
are the moral factors, influenced in turn by ideological considerations. What is so damaging is not the mere fact that men
and women desert their family duties, but rather that millions
subscribe to the doctrine of wanton self-expression. In all areas
we hear people say, "This is the free world; I propose to live
my own life as I please and nobody can stop me." This doctrine
begins by sounding like freedom and ends as moral destruc-
tion.... (YOV 85)

Deuteronomy 12:8–9   You shall not do as we are doing
    here today, every man pleasing himself—for you have not
    yet reached the resting-place and possession which the Eter-
    nal your God is to give you. (Moffatt)

29

What we need, in the Christian ministry of family life, is
some definite guiding lines, so that we may develop a con-

sistent and powerful philosophy of our vocation, sufficient to resist the temptations which, when not resisted, lead to decay. *Four* of these are especially relevant.

The first guiding line is the idea of each home as a religious institution.

A second guiding line is the frank acceptance of family life as a holy calling.

A third guiding line is the loyal acceptance of discipline.

A final guiding line is found in the idea of a home as a center of community service. (YOV 95–103)

There have been, in our history, brilliant examples of homes which were centers of new life, in that from them came new and liberating movements. Few examples are more striking than that of the home of Elizabeth Fry, who was a good mother, but from whose home came important developments in prison reform. We ought to glorify the pattern by which social vision is expected, as a result of home gatherings, and not merely as a result of gatherings of professionals or employed public officials. Thus the home may be one of the means by which the encroachment of the all-devouring state is resisted. (YOV 103–104)

Read: Proverbs 31:10–31

30

When we seek to deal with fundamental moral and spiritual questions which underlie all others, we are engaging in what, since the time of Socrates, has been called philosophy and more particularly moral philosophy or *ethics*. Accordingly this (*The Life We Prize*) is a book in philosophy, but more in the Socratic than in the professional sense. Nearly all of the moral thinking of the Western World since the time of Socrates has been established upon the conviction that there is an objective moral order so that, when we make moral judgments, we are talking about something more important and more enduring than our own subjective wishes. We believe we are talking about something that is real and therefore something about which we can make true and false statements. The alternative to this is the notion, which those on the other side of the iron curtain obviously hold, that words are merely counters in a propaganda game. Our major heritage is that of the objectivity of truth, including the truth about the good life for men. (LWP 28)

If it is true that the deepest issues of both world events and our personal lives are moral ones, it is important that we make a serious and sustained effort to describe the ideal of life which we prize. It is not enough to say that our time requires moral thinking; we must go ahead and engage in it. Of course, as a matter of fact, we do engage constantly in moral judgments, as almost any casual conversation will show. It may be noted that our popular columnists, in their attacks on one another and on public officials, regularly seek to establish themselves on high moral ground and malign one another, not for poor journalism, but for poor character. If moral judgment is inescapable, why not consider it with rigorous care? It is a sign of hope that there seems to be a shift in current mood so that a significant number of persons are now ready for such thinking, willing to engage in ethical inquiry without apology and without embarrassment. (LWP 29)

Read: Psalm 37:30–33; Jeremiah 31:31–34

31

The paradox is that our mid-century moral depression has come in the midst of better economic conditions than have been known for many years or perhaps have ever been known

anywhere. If economic factors were really the determining factors, as some philosophies hold, this could not be true, but it is.
The moral depression has not come in poverty-stricken lands,
but in the midst of almost full employment, high wages, and
abundant food. The contrast between our economic conditions
and that of the majority of the human race is so great that
we can hardly imagine it, though several able writers have
recently done their best to make us see it. (See Stringfellow
Barr, *Let's Join the Human Race.*) We understand something
of the contrast when we realize that, in Southeast Asia, the
people look upon starvation in the same way that *we* look upon
cancer; it is deplorable, but, so far, unavoidable, and thus a
necessary calamity, to be suffered without complaining. (LWP
37–38)

It might be understandable if people faced with starvation
should lose their nerve, but there is something seriously wrong
when people, living in the midst of plenty (say, in the nine-
teen fifties), go to pieces by the millions. Yet this is precisely
what is occurring in the citadel of democracy. Millions of men
and women, with sufficient to eat and to wear, and with no
experience of being bombed or made homeless, are actually
holding on in desperation, trying not to go to pieces! (LWP
38)

Read: Luke 10:25–37

32

What we seek, as we face the task of living with other people, is some guiding principle which may help to bring order
out of our daily confusion. This has been sought for centuries
by some of the best minds which our race has known and
these have left us a garnered wisdom. Frequently we have
been very slow, in our total culture, to apply with any adequacy

the principles already accepted, but the application does come at last. It took eighteen hundred years for men to see that the principle of the infinite value of every human soul made human slavery untenable, but at last the application came. It is wholly possible that there are other applications, quite as inevitable, but that we have not yet become conscious of them. The moral as well as the physical universe is wider than our view of it. (LWP 99–100)

The development of personality is something that has come late on the earth, and at the climax of a long development. The earth was in existence long before there were men on it, and likewise the earth was inhabited long before men joined the other inhabitants. Man, when he appeared, appeared in an already going world. If we follow the available evidence we must conclude that, for a long period, the earth was merely a material unit with wind and weather and tides, but no life. Vegetable life appeared first and was followed much later by animal life, with its remarkable capacity for movement and finally for consciousness, in the sense of awareness of the environment. Personality was quite as signal an advance over animal life as life itself had been over mere matter. . . . The higher levels presuppose the lower ones, but the lower do not presuppose the higher. The most striking way in which the levels appear is as follows: 1. Unconsciousness. 2. Consciousness. 3. Self-consciousness. (LWP 101–102)

Read: Psalm 8; Ephesians 4:25

33

Among those who have demonstrated the Christian pattern of wholeness, one of the most outstanding is John Woolman (1720–1772). Where others are eminent, Woolman is a giant. More than one hundred years before the Civil War, this simple-hearted man inaugurated an effective plan of immediate emancipation of slaves in America, while at the same time he wrote his *Journal* in such an attractive fashion that it has become a devotional classic. (NMOT 43)

Sensitive readers soon begin to see why (Charles) Lamb made such a strong recommendation of the writings of an unpretentious man when they note the remarkable combination that Woolman's experience represents. On the one hand, they make the acquaintance of a man who was humbly and unapologetically devout, while, on the other hand, he was clearly an activist. During the last day of his life, he called for pen and ink and wrote, with much difficulty, his final message as follows: "I believe my being here is in the wisdom of Christ; I know not as to life or death." From beginning to end, the devout man sought to live in the divine presence and to seek a wisdom not his own. (NMOT 45)

The important lesson that Woolman provides for modern man lies not in the fact that he stressed equally the life of devotion and the life of social consciousness, remarkable as that is, but rather the particular way in which the one actually led to the other. Woolman's social consciousness, concerning both the poor and the enslaved, arose, not in spite of, but *because* of his rich life of devotion. It was when he meditated deeply upon the universal love of God that he realized that each person has a moral responsibility to help all creatures to share in that love, without man-made limitations. All that we own, therefore, we own in the light of "a common interest from which our own is inseparable." We are brothers because we derive from a common Father. Our genuine vocation is to become God's instruments in the liberation of all. (NMOT 48 f.)

Read: Matthew 25:31–40; Micah 6:6–8

34

What we most need is some landmark of which we can be sure. This will not relieve us of the necessity of further searching, but it will assure us that we are moving in the right direction. . . . Being finite men we can never have absolute certainty or infallibility . . . but we may, if we are fortunate, find something of which we are so deeply persuaded that we are willing to stake our lives upon it. Such faith is not certainty or credulity, but courageous trust. (LWP 213–214)

Is there anything, in this world of doubt and probability, that you verily believe, and by which you are willing to abide though the heavens fall? There is one such in my life, perhaps the only one, but one such is sufficient. It was given marvelous expression long ago by a superlatively gifted man who supported himself by making tents, but who found both meaning and joy in his life because he was utterly dedicated to one particular cause. His words were these: "For I am persuaded, that neither death, nor life, nor angels, nor principalities, nor powers, nor things present, nor things to come, nor height, nor depth, nor any other creature, shall be able to separate us from the love of God, which is in Christ Jesus our Lord" (AV). It is no wonder that the people to whom these words were written were called those of the Way. We cannot see very far into the darkness of the future and the prospects are not really bright, but it is something if, together, we find the road. (LWP 214)

Read: Ephesians 1:15–23

II

The Idea of God

35-67

35

Any people is safe from acquiescence in wanton tyranny if it keeps closely before it the recognition that there can be only one ultimate loyalty and that the Living God is the only worthy object of such loyalty. This clears men's minds and makes them bold. Our historic religion leads not to an easy tolerance, in which all distinctions are blurred, but to the sharpest kind of distinction. Pure religion is the final enemy of all totalitarianism because the worship of God will brook no rivalry. (FFR 14)

The real believer in God, then, has a basis of action which no nontheistic humanist can ever have. If there is no ultimately valid criterion by which man's conduct may be judged, who is to say *which* human tradition is right? (FFR 18)

When men fail to believe in God in a straightforward and objective sense, they stress their own subjective experiences. Then, in place of having faith in God, they have faith in "science" or in "religion." But both science and religion are human pursuits. Therefore when we make them the objects of our veneration we are guilty of idolatry. (FFR 28)

Daniel 11:32 . . . by means of specious promises he shall pervert those who bring guilt upon the nation. But those who know their God shall be steadfast and take action. . . . (Moffatt)

Proverbs 9:10   The first thing in knowledge is reverence for the Eternal, to know the Deity is what knowledge means. . . . (Moffatt)

36

What most of us now require is a new vision of God's purpose for mankind and our part in it. Before the burst of new life which we associate with the career of George Fox in 1652, a burst which we have seen as an encouragement for us in our own perplexed time, young Fox had a vision. He was on a small mountain, in the west of England, called Pendle Hill. . . . William Penn said that Fox "had a vision of the great work of God in the earth, and of the way that he was to go forth to begin it." (AF 122)

(What Penn said of Fox) is the ecumenical idea; this is the Christian ideal. At this juncture of history it seems far from realization, but it is eternally valid. This is the clear vision which makes us know how imperfect our present condition is. Perhaps it is the vision without which a people will perish. (AF 123)

If Christ is trustworthy, God really is! I have many reasons for believing in God, but the one reason which I find inescapable is the testimony of Christ. Having made Him my center of certitude, it is not rational to refuse to follow Him in His own deepest experience and conviction. . . . (PS 59)

Romans 11:33   What a fathomless wealth lies in the wisdom and knowledge of God! How inscrutable his judgments! How mysterious his methods! (Moffatt)

37

Good as (a belief in objective morality) is, and important as it is, the emphasis on moral foundations is not enough. Law is wonderful, but, when we think carefully, we know that Law requires a Lawgiver. Of all the ideas connected with the free society, the one which is the most exciting, as well as the most fundamental, is that the Lawgiver truly is, and is not a figment of our imaginations or a projection of our human hopes. Both socialism and secularism are widely espoused as substitutes for a deep religious faith, but they are obviously inadequate if something stronger can be presented as the more reasonable alternative. (DF 113–114)

If we need something to buttress us in the inevitable struggles of life, there is nothing that can help us more than the conviction that each one of us is sought by Him who made the Pleiades and Orion, that each of us is truly known as no finite men can ever know us, and that, in spite of our feebleness and sin, we can become channels of God's universal love. Even the unjust happenings of the present life cannot dismay us, because this life is not all. If God really is, then a future life is required in order that the manifest injustices of the present life may be redressed. (DF 117)

Amos 5:8   . . . he it is who made the Pleiades and Orion, who turns black darkness into dawn and darkens day again into the night, who summons floods and pours them on the earth; his name is the Eternal. . . . (Moffatt)
Read: Daniel 12:1–4

38

The familiar statement that God cannot be proved is fundamentally ambiguous. On the one hand it may mean that the existence of the One whom Christ called Father cannot be proved beyond a shadow of a doubt, but on the other hand it may mean, and often does mean, that there is no valid evidence for the being of God. One does not need to be a professional philosopher to see that these two meanings differ radically. Part of the trouble lies in the fact that, while the writer may mean the first, the reader may interpret him as meaning the second, with the result that faith is further eroded. (PS 21–22)

The time has now come to point out that the sentence "God cannot be proved," while true, is profoundly misleading. Furthermore, it is often used in a way which is manifestly dishonest, because care is not taken to add that absolute proof is not possible anywhere else. Without the addition of this important observation, the reader is not to be blamed if he concludes, erroneously, that items of Christian faith are without support while items in other fields, such as science, have the value of certainty. (PS 22)

Malachi 3:14   You have said, 'It is useless to serve God,' and 'What gain is it to do his bidding, to walk in penitent garb before the Lord of hosts?' (Moffatt)

Jeremiah 9:23–24   A wise man must not glory in his wisdom, nor a warrior in his strength, nor the rich man in his riches; he who glories is to glory in this, that he has insight into me, that he knows I am the Eternal, dealing in kindness, justice, and goodness upon earth—for these are my delight. (Moffatt)

39

The new developments in the contemporary scene which have produced so much erosion of faith differ radically from the ancient denial of God which men expect and know how to handle. Confusion arises because there are many widely publicized systems of thought which use some theistic language, and even speak of prayer, yet in which the words when carefully examined turn out to mean something different. Some authors spread confusion by quoting the Bible while at the same time rejecting the central conception of God that Christ reveals. (PS 62–63)

Is the Christian a person who loves God, or is he one who loves his fellow men? Though the question is asked, it is really a foolish one. A Christian is one who is committed to Christ, and Christ stressed the two commandments without preference. Though there are many paradoxes in the Gospels, and though its truth cannot be rightly stated apart from paradox, there is no paradox more striking than that of the "double priority." Christ gave two "firsts." The one "first" was exactly what His hearers expected, because they were familiar with the Shema (Deuteronomy 6:4), which was repeated daily. They knew that they were required to love God and to love Him wholly. (NMOT 30)

Read: Proverbs 30:1–4; James 3:13–18

40

No one is outside the Law, just as no one is outside the Divine Concern.

Such an understanding of the nature of the human situation provides a far stronger motive for overcoming racial injustice than does any merely economic or political or legal conception. If it could be followed with any sincerity, it would provide an antidote to all racism, whether of the white or the black variety. General acceptance of such convictions would not make laws unnecessary, but it would lead to the enactment of laws, and, furthermore, help to provide some of the spirit that keeps men from circumventing laws by their own clever devices. A world in which men of different races can look upon men of contrasting color as Children of God is one in which equal freedom can come without bitterness. (NMOT 97)

A Christian is one who believes that God exists just as truly as a stone exists. The fact that God is utterly different from the stone has no bearing on whether the object of awareness is genuine or imaginary. The real alternative to existence is what is *imagined*, and if God is an imaginary Being, we may as well cease to engage in all talk about Him. The intelligent operation, then, would be to forget the subject and to go on with something pertinent to our lives. We must be sufficiently unsentimental to admit that what is nonexistent is only delusory. . . . A God who has only subjective reference . . . is far indeed from the One to whom Christ prayed as "Lord of heaven and earth" (Matthew 11:25). (NMOT 117)

Ecclesiastes 8:5–6   He who obeys the royal command will never come to harm. Still, the wise heart knows there is a time of judgment coming, even though today men may be crushed under the king in misery; for all there is an hour of judgment. (Moffatt)

Hebrews 6:1   Let us pass on then to what is mature, leaving elementary Christian doctrine behind, instead of laying the foundation over again with repentance from dead works, with faith in God. . . . (Moffatt)

41

Modern man can be helped immeasurably by the realization that at the heart of all that is, stands not mere power, but *A Person*. We have all been aware of the temptation to think of God in impersonal terms, on the mistaken assumption that this has somehow liberated us from childish superstition or, when we want to sound impressive, from what we call "anthropomorphism." The odd consequence is that in this understandable effort, we have moved down rather than up; a force is clearly inferior to a person, since a person can know a force while a force cannot know either a person or itself. A person is not a being with a body, though we, as finite persons, happen now to inhabit bodies. A person is any being, finite or infinite, capable of reflective thought, or self-consciousness, and of caring. The greatest of these is caring. (NMOT 119)

We are given a keen sense of the need of more rigorous thought on the deepest questions when we encounter persons who are trying to hold on to some idea of God, but who, at the same time, reject the personal relationship that Christ taught and illustrated. (NMOT 119)

John 4:23-24   "But the time is coming, it has come already, when the real worshippers will worship the Father in Spirit and in reality; for these are the worshippers that the Father desires. God is Spirit, and his worshippers must worship him in Spirit and in reality." (Moffatt)
Read: John 9:30-39

42

Part of the weakness of the Christian movement in our generation has been the relative lack of emphasis upon belief. There are three areas that must be cultivated if any faith is to be a living faith: the inner life of devotion, the intellectual life of rational thought, and the outer life of human service. There is no doubt as to which of these has been most neglected in our time; it is the emphasis upon rational belief. Christian books dealing with prayer and worship have been plentiful; books urging men and women to tasks of mercy have been abundant; but good books helping to arrive at sound convictions have been scarce. . . . (PS 17)

However good and important human service is, it loses its

motive power when the sustaining beliefs are allowed to wither. That mere humanistic idealism has a natural tendency to end in bitterness is not really surprising. . . . People *do* disappoint us, and if we have nothing more fundamental upon which to depend than the natural goodness of man we are bound to end in a mood of futility. The social witness of the modern Church, especially in regard to racial justice, is very important, but we need to remember that the social gospel depends ultimately upon convictions. Unless it is true that each person, regardless of race or sex, is one who is made in the image of the Living God, much of the impetus of work for social justice is removed. . . . (PS 18)

Hebrews 12:5   And have you forgotten the word of appeal that reasons with you as sons?—My son, never make light of the Lord's discipline, never faint under his reproofs. . . . (Moffatt)
Read: Psalm 119:65–80

43

We hear, repeatedly, the cliché that deeds are everything while beliefs are unimportant; but this is manifest nonsense. The truth is that belief leads to action, and acting often depends upon believing. We are wise to remind ourselves of what Dr. Johnson said to Boswell on July 14, 1763, apropos of a man who denied the existence of a moral order: "If he does really think that there is no distinction between virtue and vice, why, Sir, when he leaves our house, let us count our spoons." (James Boswell, *The Life of Samuel Johnson*, New York: John B. Alden, 1887, Vol. I. p. 346.) If men believe that slaves are not fully human they will treat them as they treat animals. A man who is convinced that something is impossible will not, if he is intelligent, try to produce it. (PS 19)

Unfortunately, the intellectual effort that modern man so desperately needs, especially in his faith, is not being generally encouraged. Instead, there is a real discouragement produced by the preaching of anti-intellectualism. . . . The consequence is that many draw the erroneous conclusion that all items of faith are devoid of intellectual support. . . . (PS 19–20)

John 20:30–31   Many another Sign did Jesus perform in the presence of his disciples, which is not recorded in this book; but these Signs are recorded so that you may believe Jesus is the Christ, the Son of God, and believing may have life through his Name. (Moffatt)

44

If there is any suspicion that our standards are of our own making, weakness is bound to set in. *Those who make can also set aside.* What we need in order to give power is not an assertion of our own ideals, but contact with the eternally real. The ideal may be our own imaginary construction, wholly devoid of cosmic support. What men need, if they are to overcome their lethargy and weakness, is some contact with the real world in which moral values are centered in the nature of things. This is the love of God, for which men have long shown themselves willing to live or to die. The only sure way in which we can transcend our human relativities is by obedience to the absolute and eternal God. (PMM 60)

It is especially in our Christian tradition that we find the power which is so conspicuously lacking in mere moralism. We must not forget that, in the Roman Empire, Christ won, and won against tremendous odds. He won because the faith in Christ really changed the lives of countless weak men and made them bold as lions. He has taken poor creatures who could not even understand the language of moral philosophy and shaken the world through them. (PMM 62–63)

I John 2:15–17   Love not the world, nor yet what is in the world; if anyone loves the world, love for the Father is not in him. For all that is in the world, the desire of the flesh and the desire of the eyes and the proud glory of life, belongs not to the Father but to the world; and the world is passing away with its desire, while he who does the will of God remains for ever. (Moffatt)

45

The average Western intellectual appears to think of himself not merely as a humanist, which we all are, but as a humanist and no more. As such he is not necessarily antagonist to religion, since there is obviously no contradiction between interest in human values and faith in God. Indeed, the main historic tradition in humanism has been Christian humanism, consciously refreshed at Christian sources. But, though the modern humanist does not oppose religion, he usually does something worse—*he ignores it.* He acts in practice as though God does not exist and, without arguing the matter, assumes rather uncritically that religion is something outgrown. The result is that much of our current humanism is atheistic in practice, though not in theory. It is supposed that the fruits of the ancient faith can be enjoyed without attention to its roots. (PMM 54–55)

The terrible danger of our time consists in the fact that ours is a *cut-flower civilization.* Beautiful as cut flowers may be, and much as we may use our ingenuity to keep them looking fresh for a while, they will eventually die, and they die because they are severed from their sustaining roots. We are trying to maintain the dignity of the individual apart from the deep faith that every man is made in God's image and is therefore precious in God's eyes. Certainly we cannot maintain this if we accept a metaphysical doctrine that refuses to admit any difference in kind between a living mind and a mechanical structure. We do not reverence a mechanical structure—we *use* it. We are trying to keep the notion of freedom, especially freedom of speech, while we give up the basic convictions on which freedom depends. . . . belief in objective truth and belief in objective right are part of what we mean by belief in God. (PMM 59–60)

Read Jeremiah 17:5–8; I Peter 4:12–16

46

Here, then, is our predicament: We have inherited precious ethical convictions that seem to us to be profound, central, and essential. But they have a curious inefficacy. *They are noble, but they are impotent.* We are amazed, by contrast, at the power that an alternative creed can engender. It is clear that something more is needed, that moral convictions, while necessary to the good life, are not sufficient. Perhaps an analysis of recent experience will give us a clue as to what this "something more" is. (PMM 51–52)

Most careful observers agree that the two systems of life which . . . inspired the youth of Germany and of Russia (as of the 1930's) are quasi-religious. They are much more than economics, and they are much more than politics. They are undoubtedly inadequate as religions, and in large measure *false* religions, but they have the effect that only religion can have. Millions now dying (1944) on both sides of the eastern front are dying for a faith. When we say that the system of which Adolf Hitler has been the prophet . . . is fundamentally religious, we mean that it includes the element of absolute commitment which is everywhere the distinguishing mark of religion. The sad truth is that this commitment can be given to base objects more easily than it can be given to the Living God. (PMM 52)

Read: Jeremiah 2:9–13; Acts 17:22–28

47

We understand much of the distinction between religion and other phases of our lives when we sense the profound difference between faith and belief. Faith is closer to courage than it is to intellectual assent. Faith is easily understood by the gambler, as both Blaise Pascal and Donald Hankey knew, because the gambler stands to win or lose by his play. This was brought out in Kirsopp Lake's now classic definition, "Faith is not belief in spite of evidence, but life in scorn of consequences." *Faith*, as the plain man knows, *is not belief without proof, but trust without reservations.* (PMM 52–53)

Moralizing cannot stand against a burning faith, even when that faith is an evil and perverted one. It is almost as ineffective as an umbrella in a tornado. The only way in which we can overcome our impotence and save our civilization is by the discovery of a sufficient faith. Goodness we must have, but the way to goodness is to find our peace in the love of God who, as the Source of goodness, makes us know that, even at best, we are not really good. This is the peace that passes understanding, though it is not a peace that negates the understanding. (PMM 64)

I Thessalonians 4:1–2   Finally, brothers, we beg and beseech you in the Lord Jesus to follow our instructions about the way you are to live, so as to satisfy God; you are leading that life, but you are to excel in it still further. You remember the injunctions we gave you, by authority of the Lord Jesus. (Moffatt)
Read: Joshua 24:16–24

48

We are far better acquainted with spirit than matter. We are mere onlookers when we note how one physical event causes another physical event, but we are participators when we *produce* a physical event or another mental event. Matter we must always observe from the outside, but we know spirit from the inside. We may not be able to know spirit by description, but that is unnecessary; we know it by acquaintance. (ESR 45)

The presence of the completely spiritual and loving God as the deepest fact of our lives, a presence which to many is a fact of experience, can neither be proved nor disproved by an appeal to the senses or an appeal to reason. The reality of God who is Spirit is neither a necessary conclusion nor an impossible conclusion. It belongs for all men to the realm of the possible, but it belongs, for some men, to the realm of the actual. (ESR 52)

One of the most enduring factors in civilization is man's interest in his own nature. Men have tried in all generations to know themselves and have been united by the nature of the problem rather than by the character of the conclusions reached. Man has long been called the reasoning animal, the laughing animal, the praying animal, and so on almost without end. More recently he has been called the metaphysical animal and the epistemological animal, but at least one fact becomes clear: whatever else man is, he is the "anthropological animal," the creature who is interested in himself. (ESR 53)

Read: Philippians 3:1–9

49

Jesus, more than anyone who lived before him, enunciated clearly the transcendent value of every individual spirit. Jesus called to all those with a human form, no matter how desolate, discouraged, or evil, and said they were important in the sight of God. Each one, in the teaching of Jesus, is a child of God, and that fact is not affected by any accident of race, nation, age, sex, intelligence, or creed. "You are all children of God," he told men, "and you are of more value than many sparrows or even the whole world." A full understanding and acceptance of this great teaching leads to a transvaluation of all values, to a recognition of the fact that it is necessary to lose your life in order to save it. This idea is older than Jesus, but who else made it so vivid and convincing? "He was the first to give it calm, simple, and fearless expression," says Harnack, "as though it were a truth which grew on every tree." (Adolf Harnack, *What is Christianity?* London, 1904, p. 70.) (ESR 60–61)

That system of life is good which sets men free, which releases divinely given powers, which provides for the nourishment of the spiritual life in all its phases. That system is evil which denies brotherhood and ceases to look on separate men as absolute ends, sacred in and of themselves. . . . Our belief in the sacredness of human life must be transmuted into a powerful love which makes us break the chains which bind men because we really care. In this way we shall gain the power to know blasphemy when it appears and to go beyond it. (ESR 154)

Read: Luke 12:4–12

50

The world view we are presenting, the world view of spiritual religions, is one which recognizes a deep and wide fissure in the cosmos. This fissure separates spirit from what is not spirit and, for the religious mind, it is the most significant chasm in the universe. Part of man is on one side of this chasm and part of him is on the other. He is the link between the two parts of the world, as the ancients said, and any sound religion will recognize clearly man's relation to this chasm. It is because he is partly on one side that he needs salvation, and it is because he is partly on the other side that he is capable of being saved. (ESR 61)

The fact that man has a sense of sin and feels the need of salvation is truly remarkable. Man's sense of sin as a spiritual blemish utterly different from a mere mistake is one of the strongest evidences of his spiritual nature and one of the most striking results of his self-consciousness. That the sense of sin is uniquely human has been well argued (cf. A. E. Taylor, *The Faith of a Moralist*, London, 1930), and it is easy to show that the implications of this sense carry us far. Above all, the sense of sin is our ground of infinite hope. We cannot advance without great needs which demand satisfaction and we could hardly have salvation if the need for it were not felt. (ESR 61-62)

Read: Jeremiah 20:7-9; Romans 7:14-25

51

The condition most nearly opposite of salvation is one of *waste*. Waste is the real tragedy in any avenue of life, and any thoughtful person is moved when he sees great powers which are either undeveloped or badly used. It is more than a truism that the saddest words are "it might have been." If every divine propensity were to be used, if no essential part should atrophy, that would be salvation. (ESR 65-66)

Salvation so conceived is something far deeper and more radical than moral change in the narrow sense of the word. Moral results follow, but the experience behind the moral change is fundamentally religious; it is akin to the supreme act of reverence or trust. There must be an inner spring behind and beneath the new conduct and this is another way of say-

ing we must be born again. The change must be internal
before it can be external. A second birth is not something for
the emotionally unstable, but is a healthy, wholesome, and
normal human experience. (ESR 66)

But how is a man saved? How can we be born anew? The
message of Jesus, as well as of countless others, is that we can
be saved only if we give ourselves away. This paradox is absolutely central to the spiritual life and may be illustrated without end. The person who is continually concerned about the
state of his soul, and the moral progress he is making, is in an
enterprise which is necessarily self-defeating. (ESR 66)

Read: Romans 8:1–11; Joel 1:8–12

52

Religion at its best is always a matter of paradox and this is
illustrated nowhere better than in the mood of worship. Wonder without trust is enfeebling, and trust without wonder is sentimental, but the two together produce a mood which is the
highest that men know. We are reminded of the height of a
great Gothic cathedral which is made possible by the fact that
the central arches and the flying buttresses push against each
other. The loftiness of worship is possible because of the thrust
and counterthrust of wonder and love. (ESR 76)

If our religious services overemphasize the intellectual aspect,
they destroy the mood of worship. It is unfortunately true that
many churches come to be places of instruction and little
more. The people who attend them may learn many facts, but
they are not likely to be caught up into a mood that elevates
them to new levels. It is obvious that conduct is often quite
unchanged by mere intellectual assent, but a general mood is
so deep-going that it must eventually affect an individual in
countless ways. It is not important that little children should

understand what is said by the minister, but it is highly important that the adults about him should be genuinely reverent,
for the mood of reverence goes over to the child, even without
his knowing it. (ESR 80)

Read: Psalm 119:1–8; Luke 4:31–37

53

That God has spoken directly to men has been accepted as
a fact by countless generations of religious persons. This is
what has been meant by the emphasis on revealed religion, as
apart from merely natural religion. Man has, indeed, had
desires and tendencies within himself which have helped to
produce what we call religion, but this is not all; at the same
time, so it has been devoutly believed, God has contributed to
the total result by His own self-revelation. The religious spirit
has not been the desire of the moth for the star, but has been
a "double search." (Cf. Rufus M. Jones, *The Double Search*,
Philadelphia, 1906.) (ESR 98)

The task of spiritual religion is to show, not that revelation
is to be denied, but to show the necessity of the extension of
the concept. It has often been assumed that God once spoke
directly to men, but the time came when this ended arbitrarily,
since which time men have only known God at second hand.
The theory of the inspiration of the Bible has been taught in
this way for generations, but the theory is not defensible. If
we accept the teaching of Jesus about the nonlocal character
of God, it is hard to suppose that God would limit the revelation of Himself to a particular time and place. (ESR 100)

The Bible, as a record of direct illumination, is a great help
to us, but not as something external. The Bible can be of real
aid only if the reader has within himself the experiences to
which the Biblical writers point. A revelation which was com-

pletely of the past would be a useless revelation, and the Bible means more if revelation is continuous. The ideal situation is that in which the inner and the outer revelations buttress, supplement, and check each other. (ESR 102)

Read: John 12:35–40; Isaiah 56:1–5

54

We tend to proceed with a spiritual naïveté, unaware of the sources of our convictions. When we extol service as the mark of greatness, we honor a humility which is more noble than pride, but seldom realize that we might not have understood that it is these very ideas that provide us with some understanding of the Maker of heaven and earth. What if the Eternal Mind, underlying all reality, were indeed the Suffering Servant, with the spirit of the little child? The astounding revelation is that this is true! (PS 55)

We have a tendency, of course, to say the words of a creed mindlessly, but the most familiar words would shake us if we were to understand them. The worshiper who says, "I believe in Jesus Christ," is really saying that the story termed the Incarnation presents the truth as abstraction can never do. To believe in Christ is to believe that God is like Him, and that is to believe that suffering love rather than sheer power stands at the center of all reality. To believe in Christ is to be convinced that suffering and long-suffering love constitute the very pillars upon which the universe is built. Important as thinking is, the deepest truth appears not in ideas but in events. (PS 56)

Read: Isaiah 53:4–6; I Corinthians 13:8–13

55

An examination of the Biblical use of the language of direct intimacy offers a deeper understanding of what it means to be a *person*. A person is any being to whom the word "thou" or even "you" can be intelligibly addressed! No one ever says "thou" to a physical object or to a principle or to a law, but God, if Christ is right, is neither a physical object nor a principle nor a law. He is, instead, One who knows us perfectly and whom we can partly know. It is highly reasonable to conclude that the ultimate source of our world, which includes persons, is personal, because persons make things, while things do not make persons. One of the major mistakes of modern man, even when he has been reverent, is that his conception of God has been too small. The only conception big enough to account for the world that we know is that of Infinite Personal Mind. In some Eastern religions, God is seen as infinite, but not personal; in the religions of ancient Greece, the gods were envisaged as personal, but finite; in the Biblical heritage, God is both personal and infinite. Skeptics may be able to dismiss ceremonies and priesthood and sacred buildings, but the Eternal Thou is a different matter. (NMOT 122)

We try desperately to be contemporary, we adapt the faith to current modes of thought in the mistaken assumption that Christian ideas are thus made more palatable. But Christians make very little impact when they engage in this strategy, because they thereby provoke no challenge. In its great periods, the Christian faith has been shocking to contemporaries, because it has challenged them by its refusal to conform. . . .
(NMOT 122–123)

Read: Psalm 63
Romans 12:2   And do not conform to the present age, but be transformed by the entire renewal of your minds, so that

you may learn by experience what God's will is, namely, all
that is that will which is good and acceptable to Him and
perfect. (Weymouth)

56

According to theism, God is completely and radically personal. By this theists mean that God is not a mere Ground of
Being but One to whom personal pronouns can be applied
with intellectual honesty. He is not an "it," or an abstraction.
Above all, says the theist, God is the One with whom it is
possible for even finite men to have an "I-Thou" relationship.
He is One who can be encountered in prayer as well as the
providential guidance of our lives. Every finite person is an
object of His infinite care, known and loved individually. This
is the conception of God that underlies, at every point, the
Hebrew and Christian Scriptures which we call the Bible. It is
the conception that dominates the recorded life and teachings
of Christ, for in Christ Biblical theism reaches its climax and
fulfillment. (PS 62)

There are many good reasons for knowing that God, far
from being a fantasy of our minds, really exists, but no reason
is more compelling than that which is involved in understanding what it is to be a person. If we, as modern men and women,
begin with experienced fact rather than with speculation, we
are wise to stress the known fact that persons actually exist.
We know this because *we* are persons. Though we do not know,
and may never be able to know, whether there are thinking,
self-conscious and partly self-directing beings anywhere else in
the sidereal universe, we know that such beings exist in this
century on one of the smaller planets, in orbit around one
particular sun. This may seem too obvious to mention, because
it is common knowledge, but it is certainly not too obvious to

examine. It is, indeed, one of the most important of all known facts. (PS 77)

Read: John 17

57

We must have an answer to the critic who says, "It is absurd to try to change the will of God, for if we believe in Him at all, we necessarily believe that He is already ordering all things for the best." We are making the beginning of an answer when we point out that the position just enunciated begs the question. Do we know enough about God's will to be sure that it is always done? As soon as we ask that question we begin to have some light. The fact seems to be that God's will is *not* always done. I have no doubt that He has a will for my life, but I am quite sure that I frustrate it time and again. The possibility of the frustration of God's will is a necessary corollary of the truth that there is a sense in which men and women are really free. Not only are we free to initiate action; we are also free to resist. (PS 88–89)

When we begin to look at the world with any genuine humility we realize that it is at least thinkable that there may be invasions into our causal system, for there is nothing illogical about the idea that God is superior to what we call natural law. We are helped along this liberating road when we realize that natural laws do not tell us what *must be*, but are mere generalizations of what, in a very short period of history, has been generally observed to occur. The Christian understands natural law as merely the way in which God's purposive action in our little corner of the universe normally takes place. When I first began to entertain the idea that there is nothing sacred about a closed system, this constituted for me a great emancipation. . . . (PS, 93)

Read: Matthew 6:6–15

58

It is apparently a serious mistake to think of God's will as something fixed and inflexible, but we make this particular mistake whenever we fall back into mechanistic ways of thinking which fail to rise to the level of the truly personal. The clue to a solution lies in the recognition that we are persons and that God is a Person. Of course it does no good to pray to a machine, but God is not a machine. He is, by contrast, the interested and undismayed Lover, and He is such because He is like Christ. This does not mean, of course, that He requires information. It is fatuous for the person who makes an inaugural prayer to inform God that the date is the twentieth of January. In the same fashion we can be sure that God already understands our hearts, our sins, our motives, our regrets. "There is not a word in my tongue, but, lo, O Lord, thou knowest it altogether" (Psalm 139:4 AV).

If God already knows what we want and, more importantly, knows what we *need*, why tell Him? Because our relationship with the Father is a personal one. Even the poor human parent wants the child to open up his heart without fear or scruples, though most of what is told is already well known. (PS 89)

Read: Luke 11:6–13

59

No Christian who understands his position settles for the sentimentality of saying that he believes in miracles because *everything* is a miracle. It sounds pious, but merely evades the issue, for it fails to face the sharp difference between classes of events. Of course each natural event, such as the birth of a baby, has about it an element of intrinsic wonder, but that is not the point at issue. Unless Christ was mistaken about Himself, the birth of *one* baby was of a totally different order, because it represented a genuine invasion of the natural order. (PS 95)

The point of this discussion is that prayer and miracle go reasonably together, because every prayer of petition is really a request for a miracle. When I pray for the recovery of my sick child, I am asking God to bring to bear upon the concrete situation something more than what is provided by antibiotics, however valuable these may be and however grateful we may be for their invention. Prayer is, in its very essence, supernatural. The communication with other finite spirits appears to be limited to the employment of sensory organs, but this is not true when the finite person is in real communication with the Infinite Person, for there is no sight, no sound, no tactile sensation. There is, moreover, no absolute limitation at all, such as the speed of light. Indeed, we are in a supernatural area of experience in which the limitations of space and time have no significance whatever. If such an area of experience is denied, the only possible conclusion is that prayer is meaningless; but if the supernatural is denied, Christ is denied, and then He is no longer our fulcrum. (PS 95-96)

Read: Acts 2:22-28

60

We do not know, and we are not likely to know, how it is possible for there to be direct communication between the Divine Mind and the human mind. Like the healed man, we can see even though we do not know the method of seeing. If we have a tolerable way of handling the problem of God's will, and if we see that the idea of a closed universe is not nearly as impressive, when examined, as it at first appears to be, we are ready to start. We are ready to see that it is not irrational

to suppose that God's cosmic purpose includes such a self-limi-
tation of His power that some events do not occur apart from
the prayers of finite men. Then, with the major barriers low-
ered, or at least made less formidable, we are ready to learn
to pray by praying. (PS 99)

If we take seriously the wisdom about entering as a little
child, our prayers need not be grand or polished. It is helpful
to know that we shall not be heard for our much speaking
(Matthew 6:7). Indeed, a great part of prayer need not involve
words at all, for words are not the music, but only the movements of the conductor's baton. As our contemporary world
becomes ever more noisy, silence is hard to find, but it can be
found if we really prize it. (PS 99)

Read: Psalm 61

61

Though paradox is always part of human life, the paradox
of contemporary existence is extreme. We have achieved
greatly, and some of our achievements have made us proud,
and rightly so. The most striking of these are in the area of
technology, culminating, for the present, in actually placing
men on a celestial body, but we have also had some remarkable successes in the social order. With these we are never
satisfied, but if we are realistic, we admit that great strides
have been made in overcoming poverty and hunger. That there
is further to go need not lead us to deny the distance already
traveled. A sense of history is helpful. (NMOT 105–106)

Central to the paradox is the fact that in spite of obvious
successes there is an obvious lack of happiness. Happiness did,
indeed, appear at the time of the first moon landing; but since
the deep malaise remains, it was only temporary. On every
side the manifest lack of laughter is so great that we may, not

inaccurately, be termed the unlaughing generation. The plight of the theater is only one of many evidences of this. Nakedness, whatever else it is, is not funny. One objective measure of our unhappiness is found in the number of individuals who in desperation turn to drugs. Nor is the problem merely economic; many of the most unhappy faces belong to those who have plenty of money to spend. The association of unhappiness and affluence requires the most careful analysis. (NMOT 106)

Luke 12:15   Then he said to them, "See and keep clear of covetousness in every shape and form, for a man's life is not part of his possessions because he has ample wealth."

62

The important observation for those who take their faith seriously is that the word "thou" is one of the most valuable words of the entire Biblical heritage. The deeper the Psalms become, the more personal they are, and the evidence of this is in the use of the second person singular. God is not One who is discussed or argued about, but One who is spoken about. "He maketh me to lie down in green pastures." But the mood changes abruptly in the fourth verse, when the reverent one says, "Yea, though I walk through the valley of the shadow of death, I will fear no evil: for thou art with me." Though this is one of the most radical changes that can be imagined, many have been so familiar with the beautiful words that they have never noticed it. What it means is that at the profoundest depths men talk not *about* God but *with* Him. (NMOT 121)

The Christian man who would be the genuinely new man that our age requires must gain new confidence. His may be a minority position, but this has occurred before, and the Christian witness has nevertheless survived. There are, of course, new dangers, but it is the vocation of Christians in every generation to outthink all opposition. There have always been predictions of the end of the Christian movement, but these predictions have been uniformly erroneous. (NMOT 126)

Read: Job 23:1-9; Psalm 139

63

The example of the Shepherd Psalm does not stand alone. It is almost impossible, for example, to miss the profound significance of the words, "O Lord, thou hast searched me, and known me. Thou knowest my downsitting and mine uprising, thou understandest my thought afar off" (Psalm 139:1, 2, AV). It is a serious mistake for modern men and women to dismiss this as being merely Biblical language, thus failing to understand that it is clearly meant to be intensely personal language. Christ echoes this when He began His most personal prayer, "I thank *thee*" (Matthew 11:25). (NMOT 122)

Almost anyone can see that if the conventional naturalism is true, God's existence makes very little difference, for He is relegated by it to a minor role. He does not, on this naturalistic thesis, participate directly and immediately in the world that He has made, but is limited by its laws. Such a God is not interesting to anyone, and especially not to the person who recognizes his need of help because of the meaninglessness of his own life. (NMOT 124)

The Christian who wishes to be truly modern will have to pay the price of rigorous thinking, for cheap modernity is transparently ineffective and really deludes nobody. Does anyone really believe that the gospel is better received if its presentation is accompanied by the use of a guitar? If contemporary prophets wish to make their maximum contribution to the improvement of society, they should try to deal, not with organizational tricks, but with exciting truth. (NMOT 111)

Read: Hebrews 6:9–20

64

Those who deny the supernatural are also obliged, in logical consistency, to deny transcendence. God, then, is limited to the world. Though it may seem odd, it is true that many who uncritically reject the conception of Divine transcendence do not go on to draw the necessary conclusion that the running down of the universe, as envisioned in the Second Law of Thermodynamics, will mean the end of God. If God is limited to the physical universe, the demise of the universe will be His demise, too. Whatever else we may say of this curious notion, we can at least point out that it is diametrically opposed to the conception of God as found in both the Hebrew and Christian Scriptures. According to the Biblical faith, while the world is dependent upon God, God is neither dependent upon the world nor limited to it. His purpose involves our human welfare, but He may have other purposes of which we are unaware and which, in our finitude, we can neither understand nor appreciate. The authentic word of transcendence is as follows: "Before the mountains were brought forth, or ever thou hadst formed the earth and the world, even from everlasting to everlasting, thou art God." (Ps. 90:2, AV) (NMOT 124 f.)

Read: Psalm 90

65

A thoroughgoing supernaturalism may be accepted by modern man, not because it provides comfort or emotional satisfaction, but because it makes more sense out of this mysterious world than does any alternative of which we know. Certainly it is not absurd. If modern man desires to be broad-minded, here is an answer to his quest. A world in which there are both nature and supernature exhibits a magnitude not offered by a world that is only natural. Supernaturalism accounts both for the orderliness of natural law, which is an exhibition of God's steady purpose, and for those occasions that we call miraculous, in which God's purpose is made unusually clear, because the unusual is required for the accomplishment of the Divine purpose. The world, then, is marked by order rather than by caprice, but the essence of the order is that of the Eternal Mind rather than unconscious law. If supernaturalism is true, as the Bible clearly teaches, natural law is neither primary nor autonomous, but is as truly derivative as is any other created thing. If natural law is derivative, it is subject to God's thought and is, therefore, not immutable. Miracle, then, is not a denial of rationality, but one of its chief expressions. If the rising of Christ from the dead was necessary for God's redemptive purpose for His world, then it was the most rational of events. (NMOT 125–126)

Read: Hebrews 3:1–11

66

The faith is indeed an anvil that has worn out many hammers. The faith that could survive in spite of the condescension of the Greek thinkers, the fierce opposition of Roman emperors, the blight of the Dark Ages, and all the challenges of the modern world, is not likely to disappear in our time. Whatever contemporary analysts may say, this is not the post-Christian age. It may be the pre-Christian age, but that is another matter altogether. (NMOT 126)

Hebrews 11:1–6.   Now faith is a confident assurance of that for which we hope, a conviction of the reality of things which we do not see. By it the saints of old won God's approval. Through faith we understand that the world came into being by the command of God, so that what is seen does not owe its existence to that which is visible (Gen. 1:1).

Through faith Abel offered to God a more acceptable sacrifice than Cain, and through this faith he had witness borne to him that he was righteous, God bearing witness by accepting his gifts (Gen. 4:4); and through his faith, though he is dead, he still speaks.

Through faith Enoch was taken from the earth so that he did not see death, and he could not be found, because God had taken him; for before he was taken he had witness borne to him that he pleased God (Gen. 5:22, 24). Where there is no faith it is impossible truly to please Him; for the man who draws near to God must believe that there is a God, and that He proves Himself a rewarder of those who seek after Him. (Weymouth)

Read: Hebrews 11:7–40

67

For Christ, and for all Christians, belief in continued life following death is clearly a corollary of belief in God. The final belief in the Apostles' Creed comes last, because it is a consequence. If God is not, then there is no reason to believe in the continued existence of finite persons and the subject is not really worth discussing. . . . But if God really is, as Christ both believed and revealed, then there is nothing strange at all about the continued existence of those who are the special objects of the Father's care. . . . (PS 111–112)

It is my deepest faith that men and women, in their fierce and faltering struggle to find the right way, are *not alone*. It is conceivable, of course, that the only point in the entire universe which has been marked by loyalty and courage and self-denial for the sake of the right, is our little earth, but I do not believe it. . . .

All this, I say, is conceivable, and if I were to learn, by some infallible means, that it is true, I believe I should try to go on living out my little day as best I might. I think I should still try to be honest and to keep my promises and to be ashamed when I failed. . . . (LWP 194)

Isaiah 25:7–8   . . . and on this mountain shall he strip away the mourning shroud from all mankind, the veil of sorrow from all nations, displacing death for evermore. So shall he wipe the tears from every face, and free his own folk from taunts everywhere ('tis the Eternal's own decree). (Moffatt)

Read: I Corinthians 15:35–58

III
Overcoming the World
68–100

68

We need to give careful attention today to the relationship between social service and evangelism. The danger is that service may take the place of evangelism or that evangelism may be redefined so that it is social service and nothing more. However desirable it may be to help workers to organize or even, in extreme instances, to strike, this does not and cannot take the place of evangelism in the sense of confrontation with Jesus Christ. The more deeply involved a person comes to be in the Christian Cause, the more he will reject simplistic approaches, and the reduction of evangelism to social action is such an approach. The early injunction of Christ was to become "fishers of men" (Mark 1:17), and this is quite as significant as the injunction to feed the hungry.... (NMOT 102)

The people who think that evangelism is dead or is fully incorporated in acts of justice and mercy would do well to think again. How is the fire of social sensitivity to be sustained and replenished? The Christian is a man who, regardless of the century in which he lives, knows the answer; he knows that the way to become ignited is to approach the Source. "Whoever is near to me," said Christ, "is near to the fire." (*The*

Gospel According to Thomas, New York: Harper & Row, 1959, p. 45.) (NMOT 102–103)

Read: I Peter 1:3–9; Ezekiel 1:10–14

69

The mood of our time is subtly marked, at all levels of society, by a keen sense of disappointment, even though it is not always expressed. Much of the basis of this disappointment is the vivid contrast between the promises and the fulfillments of our age. Never were promises so grand and never was the failure so apparent. Our people were oversold on what science and its technological products could and would do for mankind, but now even the dullest can see that these rosy promises have not been kept. One does not need to be a philosopher to realize that there can be bitterness in air-conditioned houses and that there can be gross injustice among people who go to the courtroom in fenderless cars. Even the unreflective must notice that trivialities are just as trivial when they are transmitted by the wonders of television. (SoH 18–19)

There have always, so far as we can observe, been dangerous and ruthless men, willing to destroy others if, by consequence, they might improve their own situations, but today such men can be incalculably more effective than ever before. For the first time in all history the entire population of the earth can be imperiled by ruthless men *at any point on its surface.* Every point on the earth lies within two days' travel of every other point. This is the only sense in which ours is "one world"; it is one in potential danger! The predicament of one group may, thanks to twentieth-century cleverness, be the predicament of all. (SoH 23)

Read: Isaiah 24:1–6; Isaiah 58:1–12

70

The crucial feature of our troubled world is its tragic division. More dangerous than the release of nuclear energy is the separation of the human population into two major centers of antagonistic power and conviction. Indeed, the chief reason why nuclear energy is dangerous is not because of the scientific situation, but because of the human situation. Nuclear energy would not be a threat to our race if the human population were united and friendly; in that case the peaceful uses of atomic power would be the only uses, and the brilliant technological achievements of our generation might become unqualified blessings. But this condition is far from the one which we know so well. (DF 11)

We have often, in the long story of human development, had many worlds, and sometimes we have dreamed of one world, but the awful fact now is that we have two worlds. This, which is the worst possible number, is a curiously tragic result of all our strivings to produce a civilization. After all of our years of science and government and philosophy and religion we have emerged into the predicament marked by two enormous camps, glaring at each other over artificial barriers. These two camps do not include all of the inhabitants of earth, but they include so many, and they represent such power, that all others are forced to state their own position in terms of these two. (DF 11–12)

Isaiah 19:23–25   Then shall there be a highroad between Egypt and Assyria, Assyrians passing to Egypt and Egyptians to Assyria; Egyptians and Assyrians alike shall worship the Eternal. Then shall Israel form a triple alliance with Egypt and Assyria—a blessing to the world around, and blessed by the Lord of hosts, who said, "Blessed be my people Egypt, Assyria, whom I have made, and Israel my own possession!" (Moffatt)

71

Many terms can be applied to our age, but one of the most accurate affirmations is that ours has become an age of confusion, in which people simply do not know what to think. Part of this is the result of bitter disappointment. Technology has not brought Utopia; the Great Society has not emerged; peace is as elusive as ever; poverty still exists. In no area is the perplexity greater than in that of religious belief. Millions, including large sections of the nominal membership of the churches, are without any firm conviction on which to base and rebuild their lives. It is common to hear men say that, while they once believed in God in a deeply personal sense, they do so no longer. The consequence is spiritual emptiness, a most dangerous situation. Not only is the old faith for many completely gone; there is nothing to take its place. Regardless of what statistics may report, committed Christians are today a minority, not only in Asia, but also in western Europe and in North America. To face this as a fact, and to act accordingly, is the responsibility of all who are willing to follow the path of realism. (PS 14)

We understand the Christian crisis better if we realize that the division within the general Christian community is in part a reflection of a division that occurs in the total population. Dag Hammarskjöld was speaking more accurately than he could have known, when in an address at Cambridge University in June, 1960, he said, "The human world is today as never before split into two camps, each of which understands the other as the embodiment of falsehood and itself as the embodiment of truth." We tend to apply these prophetic words to the clash between ideological groupings of nations, but they can be applied, with almost equal appropriateness, to our own citizenry. (NMOT 18)

Read: Luke 12:49–53; Micah 7:1–6

72

The most significant nonreligious division in our nation today is between those who respect and those who reject what, for want of a better term, is called the Protestant ethic. Those who accept this ethic are convinced that a man's personal conduct is important. They honor the paying of debts, fidelity to promises, and an honest day's work. Unfortunately, it is true that some of the people who live and work by this standard have insufficient sympathy for the poor, including those who are on welfare rolls. "I worked to get where I am. Why can't they?" is frequently heard. (NMOT 18)

On the other side of a deep cultural chasm are the representatives of what some call a new morality. According to this morality, it is primarily concern for the poor and for the ending of war that counts. Accordingly, a man of liberal political tendencies may neglect marital fidelity and yet be pardoned. Some, who are tolerant of infidelity and drunkenness, are not equally tolerant of participation in war. For one part of our population, the key word is honesty, for another part, the key word is compassion. (NMOT 18–19)

One of the clearest evidences of our polarized Christian mentality is the choice of hymns. The extreme pietist loves to sing, "Near to the Heart of God" and "It is Well with My Soul" while the activist, if he sings any hymns at all, prefers "O Master Let Me Walk with Thee" and "Where Cross the Crowded Ways of Life." In short, one party seeks to express and to celebrate fellowship with God, while the other party is concerned with fellowship with man, especially with those who are unfortunate. (NMOT 21–22)

Read: Colossians 2:8–15

73

Much of the current malaise is the result of a lack of integrity, in the strict sense of that term. The problem is that many of the people who, on the one hand, are devoted to permissiveness, are also devoted, on the other hand, to social justice. Frequently, the very ones who practice sexual promiscuity, because they have rejected the whole idea of a moral law, are also people who are most aroused by the alleged injustice of the military draft. But how can these go together? The truth is that they cannot go together because they are completely incompatible ideas. The resulting tension is bound to be harmful. If all is permitted, then why isn't injustice permitted? Indeed, how can injustice on this basis have any meaning at all? (NMOT 107)

If we propose to operate on the basis of ethical subjectivism, we have no right to claim that anything, anywhere, is really wrong. The systematic tolerance that recognizes both "your truth" and "my truth" leaves no room for dialogue. Why shouldn't the slave owner reply to Woolman's approach by the answer, "I like it this way?" The consistent subjectivist can have no further reply. What was to keep Hitler from claiming that persecution of the Jews was *his* truth? But if rational dialogue is logically impossible, what then? All that remains is the capacity to shout the other fellow down, or to hit him over the head with a chair, and this, in fact, is what occurs. Violence is inevitable if reason is undermined. (NMOT 107–108)

Judges 21:25   In those days there was no king in Israel, and everyone did exactly as he pleased. (Moffatt)

74

To tell the truth is never easy, for the truth is nearly always complex. Truthtelling is particularly difficult when we try to judge the current scene in the life of the West, because the tendencies are conflicting as well as varied. Ours is undoubtedly a dark time, but to say that and to say no more is to distort the truth, since ours is also an amazingly bright time. There is widespread corruption, but there is also a most heartening resurgence of thought and action *against* the corruption. Millions live self-indulgent, undisciplined lives, and even meaningless lives, but, in the midst of this, is the appearance of a neo-Puritanism as a sign, not only of moral recovery, but also of intellectual maturity. On the one hand, there is widespread loss of Christian conviction, but, on the other hand, there is the appearance of new Christian movements of astonishing vigor. (YOV 13)

Part of the paradox of our time lies in the fact that the good news arises, in large measure, from the realistic facing of the bad news. Our chief gains now come from the courageous ways of reacting to our losses. The strategy of wisdom consists in knowing so well the location of the points at which we are hard pressed that we concentrate our forces on these points and thereby actually turn defeat into victory. (YOV 13–14)

Amos 9:7–8   Are ye not as the children of the Ethiopians unto me, O children of Israel? saith Jehovah. Have not I brought up Israel out of the land of Egypt, and the Philistines from Caphtor, and the Syrians from Kir? Behold, the eyes of the Lord Jehovah are upon the sinful kingdom, and I will destroy it from off the face of the earth; save that I will not utterly destroy the house of Jacob, saith Jehovah. (ASV)

Joel 2:28–29   And it shall come to pass afterward, that I will pour out my Spirit upon all flesh; and your sons and your daughters shall prophesy, your old men shall dream dreams, your young men shall see visions: and also upon the servants and upon the handmaids in those days will I pour out my Spirit. (ASV)

75

The rebirth and wider application of the idea of vocation is a sound reason for seeing our distraught time as a time of genuine reformation. Much of the power of the Reformation of the sixteenth and seventeenth centuries arose from a rediscovery of the idea of vocation then, as men applied to common life many of the principles formerly associated with the lives of monks and nuns. Perhaps each generation needs to experience its own rediscovery of the meaning of vocation, because reformation zeal tends to dwindle. (YOV 66)

One factor (disturbing the idea of family life as a vocation) is the uprootedness of people in the industrial age. Hundreds of thousands live in trailer camps or in other temporary quarters where the stabilizing factors in family life are almost wholly absent. The people who exist in this way, moving from one well-paid job to another, often have a good deal of ready money, but they miss almost entirely the sense of belonging that can be so stabilizing. We have millions who have no real stake in the community and no membership in a group whose approbation is highly valued. Uprooted men and women do not take the same pride in family success, and when people cease to care, the family naturally goes to pieces. (RFL 18)

I John 2:1-3   My dear children, I am writing this to you that you may not sin; but if anyone does sin, we have an advocate with the Father in Jesus Christ the just; he is himself the propitiation for our sins, though not for ours alone but also for the whole world. This is how we may be sure we know him, by obeying his commands. (Moffatt)

76

That ours is a time of possible burst through the crust of history is more than a reasonable guess; it is actually beginning to be demonstrated in some areas. In no area is this clearer than in the field of religion. Though there is vast religious apathy on the part of the majority, there is intense activity on the part of a minority and it is such minorities that may be truly creative of the future. When we think of the names of the men who, near the middle of our century, have given their thought to the honest consideration of religious truth, we find a galaxy not unlike that of three hundred years ago. Not for at least a century has there been anything comparable to the contemporary virility in theology. Among the great names (as of 1950) are the following: the late William Temple, who died during the Second World War as Archbishop of Canterbury; the late Nicolas Berdyaev, long of Russia and later of Paris; the brilliant Swiss theologians, Karl Barth and Emil Brunner; the Scottish brothers, John Baillie of Edinburgh and Donald Baillie of St. Andrews; Dr. Albert Schweitzer of Africa, whose place in the affections of thoughtful Christians is unique; Paul Tillich and Reinhold Niebuhr, of Union Theological Seminary, New York; Jacques Maritain of France and America. This is only the beginning of such a list, but it is a very striking one and should be sufficient to alter the opinions of those who have supposed that vigorous religious thinking is something from a dim and distant past. (SoH 28)

John 8:31–36   So Jesus addressed the Jews who had believed him, saying, "If you abide by what I say, you are really disciples of mine: you will understand the truth, and the truth will set you free." "We are Abraham's offspring," they retorted, "we have never been slaves to anybody. What do you mean by saying, 'You will be free'?" Jesus replied, "Truly, truly, I tell you, everyone who commits sin is a slave. Now the slave does not remain in the household for all time; the son of the house does. So, if the Son sets you free, you will be really free." (Moffatt)

77

The awful truth is that our wisdom (concerning) ends does not match our ingenuity about means, and this situation, if it continues, may be sufficient to destroy us. Just at the moment of history when the technical conditions for the oneness of the globe have finally appeared, we are woefully lacking in the moral conditions that are required if this situation is to be a blessing. It is not merely that this contrast removes us from a fortunate situation; *it actually produces a situation far more evil than any formerly known. Because of lack of moral direction, what might have been a blessing becomes a terrible curse.* (PMM 14)

It is important to make it abundantly clear at this point that the crucial problem is the spiritual problem, and we here mean by spiritual that area which is the object of attention in philosophy and theology as against that area in which the object of attention is mechanical contrivance. . . . The paradox of failure at the moment of success is by no means a condemnation of technical progress, for such progress is morally neutral. It gives the surgeon's knife, and it gives the gangster's weapon. Our predicament is a commentary, not on instruments and instrument makers, but on the human inability to employ both scientific knowledge and technical achievement to bring about the good life and the good society. Man is an animal who is peculiarly in need of something to buttress and to guide his spiritual life. (PMM 16–17)

Read: Matthew 12:38–45; II Peter 2:17–20

78

The logic of the situation which the atomic bomb symbolizes is as follows. *Though the atomic bomb is the fruit of science, the solution of the problem is not a matter of science, since it is admitted that there is no technological defense. The only hope, therefore, lies in world organization. Only world organization can insure that the fearsome invention is used by those forces concerned with justice and not by lovers of irresponsible power. But since the world organization is dependent upon the trustworthiness of those concerned, the ultimate question is ethical rather than merely scientific or even political. The only answer to atomic power is moral power.* (FFR 8)

The practical task of trying to restore the foundations of our democratic civilization is so immense that all who have any gifts which qualify them for this task should give their full energies to it. Every thoughtful person now knows that the major problem of our time is the ethical problem. Even the most superficial optimist now sees that we could destroy ourselves, and that the way we use power is far more important in the long run than is the amount of power we have available. The mandatory need of our time is the discovery or recovery of an ethical creed that can give Western man, at this juncture in his history, steady moral guidance. (FFR 9)

Read: I Samuel 8:10–19

79

Fortunately, we do not need to hunt for such an ethical creed. We already have it. We already have a cluster of convictions which belong to all strands in our culture. One of the ways in which our fundamental faith can be restored and reinterpreted for our time is by an attempt to state the moral principles which have provided, in large measure, the chief standard of conduct in the life of the West for almost two millennia. Many generations have given conscious assent to these principles, and other generations have accepted them as the unconscious basis of judgment in common life. Without these principles the whole history of the West would have been utterly different. (FFR 9)

. . . this body of teaching provides material which can be taught and *ought* to be taught in our public schools. Many states forbid sectarian instruction, but this is not sectarian any more than the Twenty-third Psalm is sectarian. All children might learn:

> Above all else love God alone;
> Bow down to neither wood nor stone.
> God's name refuse to take in vain;
> The Sabbath rest with care maintain.
> Respect your parents all your days;
> Hold sacred human life always.
> Be loyal to your chosen mate;
> Steal nothing, neither small nor great.
> Report, with truth, your neighbor's deed;
> And rid your mind of selfish greed. (FFR 10)

Read: Exodus 20:1–17; Deuteronomy 5:6–21

80

It is true that our central problem is moral and spiritual. The central problem is not political, for it is clear that any political system will be destroyed if the life of the citizens has lost its meaning. It will be destroyed by war if by nothing else. The problems of world government, on which so many thoughtful people pin their ultimate hope of the abolition of

war, are really spiritual problems, since it is clear that there
cannot be world government without world community. Given
the present lack of world community, the only conceivable
effective world government would be a ruthlessly totalitarian
one. Moreover, the central problem is not the problem of science. Science can do wonders, but it cannot do what is required
(in the middle of the twentieth century). If we are interested
in noting the limits of science, we can see a revealing example
in the problem of feeding our former enemies. If we decide to
feed them, science can be of enormous assistance. It can,
among other things, provide us with hybrid seed corn and with
synthetic food or drugs. But it is not by reference to science
that we decide *whether* we are to feed our former enemies.
That is a question of quite another kind. It is a question which
concerns both mercy and justice, which constitute no part of
the scientific vocabulary. (AF 19)

Read: I Kings 22:1–28

81

It has been popular, in some intellectual quarters, to refer
to the present situation as a cultural lag in which social science
and moral philosophy have not been able to keep up with
natural science and, accordingly, to blame the moralists for
the existence of the lag. Some have said, "See, the physical
scientists have been able to make tremendous advances; the
moralists are blameworthy in that they have not kept pace."
The moralists, we are told, must be stupid and slow. Why
don't they match the physicists in brilliance? (AF 20).

This conception of the relative situation as between science
and ethics has a certain superficial plausibility but turns out
to be almost meaningless on careful analysis. Ethics and science are not comparable or equal fields but vastly and generi-

cally different. There are four important differences between them, as follows:

1. Science and ethics do not refer to two separate groups of men.
2. Both science and ethics deal with laws, but they deal with laws in radically different ways.
3. Science and ethics are not comparable or equal realms because one of them is forced to deal with freedom while the other is not.
4. Finally, the two fields are different in that one of them must face the stubborn fact of sin. (AF 20–21)

Isaiah 31:1–3   Woe to those who make their way for help to Egypt, relying on her horse, and on her force of chariots, relying on her cavalry (they are so strong!) and never heeding Israel's Majesty, never consulting the Eternal! Yet the Eternal has his own plans—doom and threats that may not be recalled; he will attack these schemers, and their evil allies. Egyptians are but men, not God, their cavalry merely mortal; let the Eternal only strike, then shall supporter and supported both collapse and crumble. (Moffatt)

82

It is hard to think of any job in which the moral element is lacking. The skill of the dentist is wholly irrelevant, if he is unprincipled and irresponsible. There is little, in that case, to keep him from withdrawing teeth unnecessarily, because the patient is usually in a helpless situation. It is easy to see the harm that can be done by an unprincipled lawyer. Indeed, such a man is far more dangerous if he is skilled than if he is not skilled. We are accustomed to this idea of moral responsibility in what we call the professions, but something of the kind is a factor in more common jobs. The house painter can cheat on his materials, the well-paid workman can squander his time.

Part of our present inflation in costs, which may ultimately be so damaging to our society that collapse follows, arises from such moral causes. (YOV 74)

The sincere application of the principle of work as a ministry would be an antidote to most of these troubles. Part of what we need in economic order is a revival of common honesty. It is conceivable that men of our time might come to take pride in meticulous care in the keeping of promises and strictness with themselves in matters of integrity. There have been periods like that before and they could come again, but they will not come of themselves. We are making a start in this direction when we give the widest possible dissemination to the idea that no amount of piety on Sunday will take the place of integrity on Wednesday. (YOV 74–75)

Read: Proverbs 11:1–12

83

We see that genuine freedom is made understandable by three relevant considerations. The first is that freedom is primarily an ethical conception and meaningless on any other basis; the second is that freedom is to be found only at the end of a process, rather than at the beginning; and the third is that the essence of that process is discipline, voluntarily accepted. The freedom we prize, in the societies that endure, is the freedom of self-disciplined men and women who have the same kind of ability to act in consideration of their fellows that an athlete has to run his race. The paradox is that the disciplined runner is far more truly free than is the undisciplined runner. The point is even more obvious in the field of artistic experience. Because I have not disciplined myself by long hours of self-control in practicing scales, I literally am not free to put my fingers on the piano keys as I now wish to do. Neither artistic nor scientific skill is possible except on moral grounds. (DF 50)

The recognition that freedom, when analyzed, turns out to be a moral ideal rather than a political one is very important for the entire war of ideas which marks our world. Apart from the whole conception of a moral order, freedom is really meaningless. Perhaps this is why communist thinkers say so little about freedom. They talk easily of peace, because peace can be presented as the absence of war, but freedom as the successful resistance of external restraint or compulsion would be incompatible both with their philosophy and their practice. (DF 51)

Galatians 4:31—5:1   Hence we are children of no slave-woman, my brothers, but of the free-woman, with the freedom for which Christ set us free. Make a firm stand then, never slip into any yoke of servitude. (Moffatt)

84

Recognizing that the two great ideas of liberty and equality are different, and that they are necessarily in tension, we must find a way in which they can be combined in practice. Perhaps each principle really needs the other, each saving the other from itself, for each alone may be damaging. Freedom without equality tends to become license, while equality without freedom produces stultification. The ideal situation is one of dynamic equilibrium in which the leading ideas of democracy balance and help one another. (DF 72)

The basic ideas of the free society all turn out, upon analysis, to be moral ideas. The free society is, in essence, the responsible society, for responsibility is the one valid alternative to both slavery and license. But responsibility is meaningless unless there is a moral order. It is utterly pointless to try to discover what it is that we ought to do, unless there is an objective standard, by which both our moral failures and our moral successes can be judged. It is idle to talk about missing the mark unless a target really exists. (DF 108)

The upholders of the free society, insofar as they understand their own position, are necessarily committed to a philosophy of objective moral value, and, in this regard, there is bound to be a fundamental cleavage between the two conceptions of life now competing for men's minds. The adherents of the free order are committed to the rule that no human being of any race or class is to be insulted or neglected, not because that is the way they like it, but because the sacredness of personality is intrinsic to the moral order which is part of the real world. (DF 108–109)

Read: Philippians 2:5–11

85

Once we understand that the free society involves a belief in objective morality, with all the attendant handicaps, we are in a far better position to present the exciting proposal to the world. Equal justice and respect for personality do not then stand alone, unsupported, but rest on a firm foundation of what is really right. They are not ideas which we can choose, but ideas which are recognized as inherent in a truly moral conception of the universe. Not only must the leading ideas be joined together for mutual support . . . ; what is more important is that all of them, once they are joined, require a common foundation in the nature of things. Only on such a foundation is there reason for hope. Our hope lies in the fact that the free society has ultimate and eternal truth on its side. (DF 113)

Amos 6:1–6   Woe to the careless citizens, so confident in high Samaria, leaders of this most ancient race, who are like gods in Israel . . . lolling on their ivory diwans, sprawling on their couches, dining off fresh lamb and fatted veal, crooning to the music of the lute, composing airs like David himself, lapping wine by the bowlful, and using for ointment the best of the oil—with never a single thought for the bleeding wounds of the nation. (Moffatt)

86

Always men have broken laws; that is nothing new. What is new is the acceptance of a creed to the effect that there is really no objective truth about what human conduct ought to be. The new position is not merely that the old laws do not apply, but rather that *any* moral law is limited to subjective reference. While this has been the position of a few individuals in various generations of the past, our time differs markedly in that this has suddenly become the position of millions. Some of them still have a slight connection with the Judeo-Christian heritage, but the obvious conflict in convictions will, if it continues, finally dissolve even the mild connection that still appears to exist. If there is no objective right, then there is not even the possibility of error, and intellectual and moral confusion are bound to ensue. The most frightening aspect of this situation is the degree to which it renders the masses vulnerable to some new dogmatism which may arise. This will not be Hitlerism, since that has been fully discredited, but something like it may again succeed if the people have nothing better than their own subjective whims to oppose to the new creed. After all, Hitler had his own "thing." (PS 15–16)

Read: Luke 11:14–26

87

In no part of our culture is the paradoxical combination of loss and gain more striking than at the spiritual center of our common life, the Christian cause. Perhaps there are always both losses and gains, but in our time both have been accentuated fantastically. The perennial situation is, no doubt, that of Ephesus in which the Apostle found, at the same moment, "A wide open door" and "many adversaries" (I Corinthians 16:9), but in our day the door is extra wide and the adversaries are unusually successful. The Christian gains of our generation are many, . . . but it is the part of wisdom to concentrate attention first of all upon our dangers and our losses. In any case this procedure helps to keep us honest and to avoid the self-delusion of easy optimism. (YOV 14)

The gravity of the loss to Christendom which the current revolution in China (1950) entails is now beginning to dawn upon our people. For the Christian movement to be forced underground throughout many parts of a nation of four hundred fifty million people, itself the chief nation of the modern missionary movement, is sobering indeed. (YOV 14)

Proverbs 11:14   For lack of statesmanship, a nation sinks; the saving of it is a wealth of counsellors. (Moffatt)

II Timothy 3:1f.   Mark this, there are hard times coming in the last days. For men will be selfish, fond of money, boastful, haughty, abusive, disobedient to their parents. . . . (Moffatt)

88

There are institutions which have never renounced, on paper, their Christian connection, but in practice are almost wholly pagan. Their leaders are afraid to take a forthright

Christian stand, for fear that they might thus seem to lose their position of academic "objectivity," and they give advancement to instructors who take advantage of their positions by ridiculing whatever faith their young students may have. At the same time a sentimental reference to the Christian *background* is still printed in the catalogue. (YOV 17)

The gravity of the loss (of our former commitment affirmations) is something which it is almost impossible to exaggerate. Christian forces once controlled these institutions of enormous potentiality and then slowly *gave them away*. In most cases the loss of this province had been made to appear in the guise of virtue. The institutions were supposedly "liberated," but the consequent freedom is not always attractive or beneficent to anyone concerned. In many situations all that is achieved by the liberation is the "freedom" of a ship which has lost both anchor and rudder and consequently drifts, the victim of any wind that blows. Great scientific work is done by humble and honest men in most institutions of higher learning, but these men are often deeply discouraged by the degree to which the institutions they serve have become places of luxurious and meaningless lounging, in a situation almost wholly devoid of a sense of greatness. As the province of higher education has been lost, it has moved in the direction of pretentious triviality. (YOV 17–18)

Read: Ephesians 4:10–15; II Timothy 3:14–17

89

One of the chief reasons why a change is setting in, so far as lower and higher education are concerned, is the pragmatic one that the results achieved by severing the cultural roots are not really attractive. In eliminating the Christian center of our education we soon found that we had eliminated much else at the same time. It is no accident that some of the worst examples of corruption during the past two years (1949–1951) have come, not in government or business, but in *colleges*. The pagan philosophy is not really so appealing, when it is applied with logical consistency. The substitution of the stadium for the chapel, as the focal point of education, is not an unqualified success. (YOV 19)

Another province which is largely lost, so far as the Christian faith is concerned, is that of the intellectuals. It is a striking fact that so many of the intellectual fads and fancies of our time have been logically incompatible with a vital Christianity. If they are true, then the gospel is false. Characteristic movements, marked by this radical incompatibility, are *behaviorism* in psychology, *ethical subjectivism* in sociological thinking, *mechanistic philosophy* in some branches of natural science, and *logical positivism* in all areas of thought. (YOV 19)

Isaiah 26:1–4   On that day this shall be the song for Judah's land: "Ours is a strong, sure city, safe with walls and ramparts set by Him; open its gates for the upright, for folk who keep the faith. Thou dost protect and prosper steadfast souls, for they rely on thee. Always rely on the Eternal, for the Eternal's strength endures. . . . (Moffatt)

90

In order to develop an affirmative faith we must present and demonstrate a conception of human life that is more exciting and more appealing, especially to the submerged peoples of the earth, than the one which now dominates minds beyond the curtain. In short, there is no chance for us unless we have a *gospel*, but a gospel is what we are most inept in producing. We find it far more difficult to produce than a new machine, a bomb, or a football formation, partly because the very idea of a gospel is slightly embarrassing. Only the do-gooder has a gospel, and who, in America, wants to be known as a do-gooder? An idealist is almost as unpopular as a fellow traveler. (YOV 23)

What is so sobering to us is the recognition that even this faith, which is literally our only hope, shows so many signs of dullness and decay. The salt, which was designed to preserve the world from decay, has not wholly lost its saltness, but in many areas it has been so adulterated that little effectiveness is in evidence. The early Christians, who had been severely beaten and admonished to keep quiet, proceeded with their public and private witness without the loss of a single day (Acts 5:42), but their modern successors are satisfied if they go to church on Easter. (YOV 25)

Habakkuk 2:4   Yon impious man! his powers shall fail him; the good man lasts and lives as he is faithful. (Moffatt)
Romans 1:16–17   For I am proud of the gospel; it is God's saving power for everyone who has faith, for the Jew first and for the Greek as well. God's righteousness is revealed in it by faith and for faith—as it is written, *By faith shall the righteous live.* (Moffatt)

91

What we need is a burning and passionate faith to which we can give ourselves. We cannot do much about the other side of the iron curtain, but we can do a good deal about *this* side and the need here is apparent. The contrast which exists between our lethargy and the burning zeal of the young leaders of China (1950) is sobering to contemplate. Though we make commencement speeches about democracy, we certainly are not aroused about it as the young communists are aroused by Marx-Leninism. The difference lies in the fact that democracy, as we ordinarily understand it, is little more than a political system, whereas Marx-Leninism is vastly more; it is a religion. Only a religion can arouse men and women as we need to be aroused and the only religion which has the slightest chance of performing the required miracle is a revitalized form of the Judeo-Christian faith, which has proved its ability to save men and civilization in other times of crisis in nearly two thousand years of troubled history. The basic Christian faith, shorn of its denominational impediments, is, in sober truth, the only known force that is more than a match for the passionate zeal which the Marxian gospel has been able to inspire during the years. A revitalized faith would not save us from strain, but it might enable us to live nobly in the midst of the strain. (YOV 24–25)

Read: Acts 14:25–27
Isaiah 7:9b   If your faith does not hold, you will never hold
    out. (Moffatt)

92

It is very clear we must keep the major emphasis, not on particular methods, but on the total enterprise. We are pointing toward higher goals. We are concerned for the revitalization of the Christian movement, by bringing to its assistance a largely unexploited human resource, the ministry of lay men and lay women. If we try to do a little thing, we shall accomplish essentially nothing. Our only hope lies in making big plans, in undertaking to produce a radical change, in aiming high. (YOV 124)

The penetration of the whole earth by the ideal of a free society would bring to an end the tragic division of the world and it would bring it about in such a way as to be beneficent to all parts of mankind. It is, accordingly, the only solution which those who care about the human race, and care realistically, can accept. Therefore, it is the first order of business for really thoughtful minds. *It is not an idle dream, but the only practicable alternative to a continuing nightmare.* This solution may be slow and it may be costly and it is a task in which we may fail, but we must undertake it because there is no other way that is compatible with human dignity. It is a hard road, but it is really the only road. (DF 17)

Read: Matthew 28:17–20; Acts 1:6–8

93

Our world is more shaken that it has ever been in our lifetime. What faces us is something far worse than a series of military reverses or even military dangers; we are faced with a widespread shattering of confidence. The world which once seemed so secure now appears to be breaking up before our very eyes. So great is the change that the crises of the first two World Wars seem simple by comparison. (LWP 15)

Another rude shock has come to us in the reluctant recognition that even our physical power is not as overwhelmingly effective as we have been led to suppose it might be. The fighting in Korea was a warning to all nations which rely heavily on industrial power, in that it showed that mechanical weapons are no match for millions driven by fanatical zeal, no matter how misguided these millions may be. When the Chinese Communist soldiers went into withering fire, wave after wave, walking over the dead bodies of their comrades, man discovered a limit to the deterrent effect of modern weapons. Even preponderant air power could not turn, for a long time, that fanatical tide. We have been taught, in our reliance on technology, to think that bombs and planes are always decisive factors in the struggle for survival, but this need not be true and, in fact, *is* not true when peoples are so inflamed that they go on a crusade, spending their lives willingly and recklessly. What is so hard for us to realize is that they are willing to crusade against *us*. (LWP 17–18)

Read: Habakkuk 1

94

Our deepest shock of all is the realization that the peace for which we have worked and fought and sacrificed has not come. We are now forced to admit that neither the first nor the second World War ever ended and that what we are experiencing (1945–1950) is only a new phase of the human turmoil of this century. But the speed of history moves ever faster, so that, whereas the period of relative quiet between the first two phases was about twenty years, the comparable period we have recently ended was a bare five years. So rapidly have the forces of history moved, that the whole Western World now has something of the insecurity which was symbolized so tragically by the quandary of France in 1940, when the Maginot Line was threatened. We have been driven out of all safe nests. Every literate person at last realizes that the things we most prize are now held in constant jeopardy. (LWP 19)

If we make moral integrity our ideal we may thereby influence, in far-reaching ways, our political decisions. It will be an evidence of our honesty if, in our attack on Russian totalitarianism, we are equally opposed to it when, by virtue of geography, it happens to be *on our side*. There is, for example, no evidence that life in Spain is much better than life in Russia and, in any case, it is far from the life based on the four freedoms. We cannot, with integrity, denounce restrictions on freedom, when they occur in Russia, and condone them when they occur in lands which might be strategically useful to us. Free-

dom, we must remember, *can* be denied on both sides of the
iron curtain and *is*. (LWP 24)

Read: I John 4

95

Our moral depression is a scandal because it shows so strik-
ingly the hollowness of our high pretensions. Our pride in
making ingenious things is deprived of all justification if, in
making the things, we lose that for which the things are made.
A sobering illustration of this paradox of failure in the midst
of success is provided by the great city of Detroit, which, in
so many ways, stands before us as an exaggerated symbol of
modernity. Insofar as ours is an age of the internal combus-
tion engine, Detroit is the key city of the planet. In this city,
cars that are truly marvelous productions are turned out with
almost incredible speed, but what of the men who make them?
We know something important about our age when we know
that the local name for the office of the big motor companies
is "ulcer alley." The stomach ulcer is one of the chief symp-
toms of our particular depression. It humbles our pride to face
the fact that we who are so clever at making machines are
often failures in the more important business of the personal
lives, by whom and for whom the machines are made. (LWP
38–39)

II Corinthians 4:7–11   But I possess this treasure in a frail
vessel of earth, to show that the transcending power belongs
to God, not to myself; on every side I am harried but not
hemmed in, perplexed but not despairing, persecuted but
not abandoned, struck down but not destroyed—wherever I
go, I am being killed in the body as Jesus was, so that the
life of Jesus may come out in my body: every day of my
life I am being given over to death for Jesus' sake, so that
the life of Jesus may come out within my mortal flesh.
(Moffatt)

96

The reason that millions actually welcome war, whatever they may say, is that war gives significance to little lives. In wartime the work of the farmer, of the mechanic, and of so many others suddenly takes on significance because each job seems necessary to final victory. This tells us something very important about human life and something which must be considered in the development of any lasting social or economic system. *Man can bear great physical or spiritual hardship, but what he cannot bear is the sense of meaninglessness.* We must find some way in which our lives count, in which they seem important, or we go mad. The ultimate enemy is not pain or disease or physical hardship, evil as they may be, but our *triviality.* What is terrible for men and women is the conviction that they are not needed, that they contribute nothing, and that their lives add up to no enduring meaning. (LWP 49)

If we accept the experience of freedom, in the sense of self-determination, as part of the truth about the world we are bound to be disturbed in mind. We cannot, then, blame all of our acts upon our childhood conditioning or upon the unavoidable influences of the external environment. Consequently we shall restore the uneasy conscience, which spurns the convenient way of escape from responsibility. It is one of the marks of a good man, as indeed it is the mark of a fully *mature* man, that he should be willing to stand up and say, "Yes, I did it. I am ashamed, but it was I who made the decision. I hope I may do better next time." If this tough-minded temper were to become general in our society we should be in a far more fortunate position than the one which we now hold. (LWP 72)

Read: Isaiah 6:1–8

97

It is time to use plain language and to admit that our popular cult of freedom is a silly cult. What we mean by freedom is lack of all restraint, inner or outer, and we ought to be wise enough to know that no good life comes that way, whatever the field of endeavor may be. We ought to have known this all along, in view of the powerful object lessons provided by both science and art. It is well known that no trustworthy science is possible without the careful discipline of the scientist's hand, eye, and brain. Indeed, the only satisfactory definition of science is a definition in terms of discipline, since science is obviously more than a body of doctrine. Science is a *method*, and the person to be trusted in it is the disciplined person. The undisciplined do not see what is to be seen through either microscope or telescope. The person without the requisite discipline cannot even read what the electron microscope says; much less can he prepare the thin sections which the instrument requires. (AF 87)

Against (the) Jewish background of the philosophy of freedom, Christian thought, beginning with the New Testament, has worked out a conception of freedom which elaborates the central paradox. Only those who have accepted some bondage are really free, we are told repeatedly. Freedom may be the moral goal, but it cannot be achieved directly; it must be earned. The mistake of so many in our generation is the fallacy of simplicity; they want freedom easily and cheaply, but they learn finally that it cannot be had in that market. What they get, instead, is a spurious article, which keeps them in permanent bondage to the passing appetites of the moment. (RFL 50)

Read: Romans 8:20–21; Psalm 119:45

98

The upholders of the free society, insofar as they understand their own position, are necessarily committed to a philosophy of objective moral value, and, in this regard, there is bound to be a fundamental cleavage between the two conceptions of life now competing for men's minds. The adherents of the free order are committed to the rule that no human being of any race or class is to be insulted or neglected, not because that is the way they like, but because the sacredness of personality is intrinsic to the moral order which is part of the real world. (DF 108–109)

We have not advanced very far in our spiritual lives if we have not encountered the basic paradox of freedom, to the effect that we are most free when we are bound. But not just any way of being bound will suffice; what matters is the character of our binding. The one who would like to be an athlete, but who is unwilling to discipline his body by regular exercise and by abstinence, is not free to excel on the field or the track. His failure to train rigorously and to live abstemiously denies him the freedom to go over the bar at the desired height, or to run with the desired speed and endurance. With one concerted voice the giants of the devotional life apply the same principle to the whole of life with the dictum: *Discipline is the price of freedom.* (NMOT 69)

Romans 6:15–18   What follows, then? Are we 'to sin because we live under grace, not under law'? Never! Do you not know you are servants of the master you obey, of the master to whom you yield yourselves obedient, whether it is Sin, whose service ends in death, or Obedience, whose service ends in righteousness? Thank God, though you did serve sin, you have rendered whole-hearted obedience to what you were taught under the rule of faith; set free from sin, you have passed into the service of righteousness. (Moffatt)

99

The way out, for modern man, is to learn to live well, not apart from the strain but *in it.* Our line of advance is not away from the storm, but through it, in the mood of the men who have flown the North Atlantic so successfully every day during the fifties. What we require is not a formula for peace, which, humanly speaking, is impossible, but rather *a formula for living wisely and well in the midst of continuous strain.* (LWP 42)

The continued and increasing strain under which life must be lived in our time is essentially the same for all, but the reactions of different persons to it differ radically. It appears that the most common reaction is that of some form of escape, and especially the effort to escape responsibility. Times are bad; indeed they are so bad and the problems so enormous, that the individual feels utterly helpless; there seems to be no place where he can take hold with any effectiveness. In that case, he argues, he might as well save his energy. Moreover, the care of great matters is the responsibility of our public men; that is what we elect them for. (LWP 59)

Read: II Samuel 12

100

Real fellowship is so rare and so precious that it is like dynamite in any human situation. Any group that will find a way to the actual sharing of human lives will make a difference either for good or ill in the modern world or in any world. But fellowship is always more likely to be genuine if men are united *for* something. The problem of purpose, however, really solves itself, so far as our discussion is concerned. Those who see the danger in which our civilization lies and who have some intimation of the spiritual renewal without which our present order cannot possibly be saved have a ready-made purpose to draw them together. What we want is a group so devoted to this purpose and so tightly organized that it can work as effectively for redemptive ends in our time as the first Christians worked for redemptive ends in the first century of our era and as the Nazis have worked for divisive ends in the first century of their would-be era. (PMM 101)

If modern man can be made to see and understand the predicament he is in, that very recognition may be amazingly salutary. As a fitting conclusion (for the reader), nothing better could be found than some of the sentences that Lord Tweedsmuir wrote just before he died, words that seem to the author to be the true conclusion of the matter. "I believe—and this is my crowning optimism—that the challenge with which we are now faced may restore to us that manly humility which alone gives power. It may bring us back to God. In that case our victory is assured. The Faith is an anvil which has worn out many hammers." (PMM 105)

Acts 4:8–12   Then Peter, filled with the holy Spirit, said to them: "Rulers of the people and elders of Israel, if we are being cross-examined today upon a benefit rendered to a cripple, upon how this man got better, you and the people of Israel must all know this, that he stands before you strong and well, thanks to the name of Jesus Christ the Nazarene whom you crucified and whom God raised from the dead. He is the stone despised by you builders, which has become head of the corner. There is no salvation by anyone else, nor even a second Name under heaven appointed for us men and our salvation." (Moffatt)

Yokefellows: A Movement from the Meditations

by Stephen R. Sebert

The many deep and delightful characteristics of Elton True-blood are partially listed in his autobiography *While It Is Day*. In it he has eight one word chapter headings: child, student, teacher, author, minister, Yokefellow, father, rambler. These descriptive aspects are not chronological, and correctly so. He still possesses a childlikeness. His zest and hope are seen in the way he encourages the sale of his books because he believes what he writes rather than a desire for profit. In fact the cost of his books is reduced by his asking for lower royalties. The student, teacher, author, and minister combine in such a way to make the first Yokefellow. It was no desire to imitate Samuel Johnson, but an acknowledgment of his own desires and life which entitled the final chapter, "Rambler." This aspect of his life is best highlighted by his smiling admonition in several meetings, "Hurry up and retire." Since his retirement from Earlham College in 1966 his many travels seem to increase annually. The seventy-fifth year of his life may be the most traveled. It is not finished as this book goes to press.

One characteristic recognized by those who know him and one he recognized in Jesus Christ is humor. The book, *The*

Humor of Christ, is almost one of its kind. Trueblood through storytelling displays the ways life makes us laugh, especially at ourselves and our attempts to be more than we are. During the revolutionary sixties he told his students one of the primary inadequacies of the so-called radicals was their failure to laugh or smile. "One might think their purpose being so serious made it impossible to laugh. All the more reason to learn to laugh," Trueblood would reply. "We must always remember we are part of the problem also. We must laugh at ourselves and with each other or we soon take ourselves too seriously." Trueblood's humor reminds him, and us, that though our mission be holy we all too often are not. The One who came on the most serious of purposes put a smile on the face of God.

Within the confines of these pages our purpose is to challenge you to consider a characteristic of Trueblood's life he does not describe in *While It Is Day*. It is for those of us who listen to discern the Voice of the Prophet. Ultimately it belongs to the One for whom prophets speak. Some believe a prophet must be dressed in strange apparel and be a totally discordant voice. They may have forgotten Isaiah's position with the king. It is also true that prophets make mistakes, often large ones, by virtue of their visibility and their claims to be in relationship to God. No claim is made to perfection or an elevation of this man unattainable by others, except for the unique God-given mission open to each person. John W. Gardner warned us in *Self-Renewal* that the smart revolutionaries choose not to warn us by external signs of dress or habit but the real radicals move us toward their goal as one of us. The measure of the modern prophet is not by the amount of ink spilled but lives and communities captured or changed by the vision.

The growth and unfolding of the heart and mind of Elton Trueblood more than hint at a vision of society renewed, although the major tool he uses in addressing this age is understatement. He tells of this vision, rightly influenced by his

Quaker heritage and the American dream, in *While It Is Day* (pages 101, 102); in 1943 he had an experience in which

as though illumined by a great light, I saw that He (Christ) did not ask for admiration, He asked for commitment! To the perplexed, the confused, the distraught, He said and still says, "Come unto Me." In all the relativities of this world there is, if Christ is right, one solid place. He offers "rest," not in the sense of passivity, but in that of a place to stand, a center of trustworthiness in the midst of the world's confusion. When I suddenly realized that my one central certainty was the trustworthiness of Christ, my preaching took on a new note of confidence, which I tried to convey to others. . . . without intending to do so I had become an evangelical Christian.

This experience did not soften the challenge to the culture as many evangelical experiences seem to do. It intensified and strengthened it. The immediate and popular response to his writings and ministry reaffirmed his experiential insight into Christ and culture.

The meditations of Trueblood display since that time a movement toward a vision far beyond fulfillment in his time. In fact at times, because of the problem of sin, it may appear the vision was an illusion. But the prophet was never called to be successful. His call is faithfulness to the voice within and the task without. The sounding of a call is his task in spite of all obstacles placed in his path by others and the inevitable weaknesses of the messenger sounding the call. Because he still encourages a deepening commitment to Christ and a broadening fellowship, these evidence his faithfulness.

One visible response to his call is Yokefellows. The emergence of Yokefellow and his extensive influence throughout the Renewal Movement are partial witnesses to his ministry. Several of the current authors and leaders in Renewal experienced the friendship and vision of Trueblood early in their careers. Keith Miller, David Haney, and Robert Raines all were encouraged and occasionally goaded to write by the persistent patience of this man. The means of measuring influence does not exist. But the Renewal Movement would be less based on the lessons of history and Scripture without his presence. Because of the difficulty and the immensity of the task the part of the Renewal Movement presented in this book is limited to the Yokefellow Movement. This presentation of Yokefellows is merely a sketch to call attention to the beginnings of a movement, to reach and capture the mind and heart of modern man as did the brothers and sisters of previous ages.

The Yokefellows arose from Trueblood's sounding a call in his writings and travels. Wherever you find Yokefellows it can be traced to the influence, at least initially, from the response to that call. This movement seeks to nurture Christian commitment, spiritual discipline, the ministry or vocation of every person, and the needed fellowship to maintain its purpose. That these expressions of the Christian faith cannot be increased with a haphazard or a general appeal is taught in Yokefellows. The weakness of the revivalistic method has been its general appeal. The principles as preached are correct. The disciplining process does not become personal enough to make a convert a growing disciple. The Yokefellow groups provide a way of deepening or personalizing the daily encounter with Christ in each other.

This method is as ancient as Christ. Trueblood wrote prolifically on this subject; *The Company of the Committed*, *The Incendiary Fellowship*, and *Confronting Christ* all provide amplification of the way Christ called from the crowd a few persons and based His church on their relationship to Him and each other.

In the final chapter of *The Predicament of Modern Man*, while calling for this redemptive society and looking at how Hitler swayed the world with just a few committed followers, Trueblood outlines what became his major mission. He wrote, "The problem is to find them, to unite them, and to make them into an effective organization cutting across all existent barriers."

The task of the prophet is to find them and make sure he does not stand in the way of those who respond. Another responsibility is that those who respond follow the message and not the prophet himself. The best way to accomplish these tasks from the experience of Biblical prophets seems to be to sound the call and provide a forum, then let the hearers choose their own response. It appears this has been Trueblood's intent. The major task of uniting and making those who have responded into powerful, highly visible instruments of Renewal remains for the following generations.

Many persons with vision never see the fulfillment of their endeavors. This apparent failure could not be attributed to their own frailities no matter how evident. The scope of the endeavor makes it impossible for one generation to overcome the accumulated sins of their fathers, but the believer makes a start. Paul's vision of a day when every knee should bow and every tongue confess appears to be far removed from even the present. But we need the persons who with prophetic eyes envision a new day. *The Future of the Christian* tells of a startling, hard-to-believe proposal: we are early Christians, not the last. Those sent to sound a call must not be required to insure a successful response. Those who hear the call are given this opportunity.

The search for Yokefellows really began in the final years of Trueblood's chaplaincy at Stanford University, although the name Yokefellow remained undiscovered. While at Stanford he reflected on the monumental needs of our civilization. The proposal of a radically different kind of fellowship existing across religious lines sounded difficult, but needed. The proposal also stimulated numerous attempts at incarnating the concept. These experimental "cells" or tiny redemptive societies gathered in factories, churches, and colleges. Many were short-lived because of the transient nature of our society, but many failed because their purpose in Renewal was limited to themselves. In his autobiography Trueblood attributes their inadequacies to not understanding a disciplined order and the universal ministry.

The symbol of the yoke and the name Yokefellow came into existence while Trueblood was traveling to Cleveland, Ohio. There he was to preach at the First Baptist Church on May 1, 1949. As he read his morning devotions from Matthew 11:28–30 the power of the symbol of the yoke came to him with such strength the sermon for the morning was scrapped and a new message came rapidly to his mind. This event in 1949 and his move to Earlham College in 1946 can now be seen as providential. At the time the move from Stanford University to Earlham College was at least a step down. That move freed him for thinking and ministry earlier than most professors.

The ten books written during the initial stages of the search for Yokefellows develop the depth and breadth of the vision. The first public phase of Yokefellows began with the publication of *The Predicament of Modern Man* and closed with the establishment of the first actual Yokefellow organization in 1954.

The first book written specifically to reach lay persons still stands as the best introduction to the total purpose of Yokefellows. *Doctor Johnson's Prayers* (1945) exhibits the literary scope and devotional desires of the first Yokefellow. *Foundations for Reconstruction* (1946) and *The Declaration of Freedom* (1955) outline the practical and political implications of a renewed civilization. *Alternative to Futility* (1948), *Signs of Hope* (1950), and *The Life We Prize* (1951) describe rays of hope and present further delineation of the needed disciplines. *The Common Ventures of Life* (1949), *Your Other Vocation* (1952), and *The Recovery of Family Life* (1953) describe the personal nature of renewal and the needed changes in our inner attitudes which result ultimately in profound political change.

These ten books were crucial to the growth and interpretation of a vision. The rooting of this new movement in Scripture, history, and sound thinking would determine its redemptive nature. The response to the proposals and ideas in the books opened many doors. One door which still bears fruit was a series of meetings across America sponsored by The Home Mission Board of the American Baptists. Trueblood distributed many yoke pins on this tour while voicing the need for Renewal. The people who heard, asked for more than a description of a possibility. Now by their letters and requests for additional guidance the time had come for a yoking of the first Yokefellows. This relationship must not violate commitments to the various denominations or it would initiate a change of loyalty not envisioned in Renewal. Yet adequate organization was needed to facilitate Renewal. The men asked to serve on the first board were Paul Davis, Edward F. Gallahue, Robert Greenleaf, Edwin Howe, Carl Lundquist, Dr. H. Vaughan Scott, and Elton Trueblood. The situation in 1953 required the board to constitute itself in such a way to continue the search for Yokefellows and create a means of nurture to lead the emerging movement desiring to be an order.

The first Yokefellow organization came into existence January 1954. Yokefellow Associates then asked Elton Trueblood, ten years after describing the predicament of modern man, to lead Yokefellows toward an embodiment of the unfolding of a prescription now called Yokefellow. Along with a number of other lay Renewal movements, Yokefellows arose to lead the church in a cleansing of the American dream and a renewal of the city. Faith at Work, Christophers, The Disciplined Order of Christ, Lay Witness Missions, and the lay departments of church councils also received a new impetus during this period.

The Yokefellow Associates held the first Yokefellow Conference in April 1954 at Earlham College. This annual conference still meets at Earlham with the same twenty-two-hour format. The board soon realized an institute was needed, also a director named because Trueblood remained at Earlham as Professor of Philosophy while serving as president of the Associates.

The insight of Robert Greenleaf, then with American Telephone and Telegraph Company, sparked the creation of the first Yokefellow Institute. The purpose of this institute was to become a center for the renewal of society through the church. The center began as a place and a people providing inspiration and expertise, the expertise in practical ways to influence the church and community. The search for persons willing to be yoked to a great vision would continue. But the momentum called Yokefellows decided to become a movement when a board was formed, an institute begun, and a director called. Now the second stage of a long pilgrimage began.

The appointment of Samuel Emerick as the first director of Yokefellow Institute became effective June 1957 and provided seventeen years of stable and imaginative leadership. This crucial position became even more apparent with the birth of other institutes. The motherhouse and her leaders set the pace.

The many types of retreats, conferences, seminars, and workshops revealed the genius of the yoke. These events exemplified the ways the inner life of devotion, the intellectual life of rational thought, and the outer life of human service are interrelated. The ecumenical character of these events brought hope to ministers and lay persons that a way could be found to minister to the total needs of a person and a community. The leadership of the program of the center was planned to expose interested lay persons to the finest minds and strongest challenges available in the total church. Persons like George Buttrick, Bishop Richard Raines, Robert Raines, Franklin Littell, John Oliver Nelson, John Casteel, Sam Shoemaker, Mary

Cosby, Elmer Homrighausen, and many others for nearly two decades have challenged lay persons by their presence and vision. A personal encounter with these persons encouraged life-changing decisions not available by reading a book. Yet many books were sold, especially after meeting the author. The books proved to be an important ministry. The bookstore of the Institute became a helpful way to introduce friends and the local church to new models of Christian education.

At the institute you could meet new ideas still in the early stages. The joy and hope of newness brought by outstanding Christian leaders invigorated a considerable number of local churches. The Church of the Redeemer, Baltimore, Maryland; Carmel Friends Meeting, Carmel, Indiana; First Presbyterian Church, Fort Wayne, Indiana; Trinity Lutheran Church, Lancaster, Pennsylvania, represent a cross section of churches mentioned in the Yokefellow Newsletter in 1961.

Ecumenicity has a direct relationship to internationalism. Two international church leaders who came consistently to share their ministry and vision of the place of the church in the world were Hans Rudi Weber and William Gowland. Weber, director of the Department of Laity for the World Council of Churches, brought an ideal representation of Yokefellows with his knowledge of the Bible combined with an ability to speak to business people. Gowland, principal of Luton Industrial College, Luton, England, headed a combination of a college and a church devoted to making the Christian faith and practice relevant to lay men and women. The areas of emphasis at the Luton College are business, industry, and commerce. Gowland provided the initial impetus for Richmond Industrial Mission. This ministry provided a forum for management and unions to speak to churches, also for the church to provide chaplains for factories in Richmond, Indiana. The international visit encouraged, paradoxically, a local ecumenical forum for Richmond.

The first institute, even in its architecture, provided a model for Christian education. The model building was a combination of worship and recreation areas, a bookstore, a library, eating and sleeping rooms, which caused people to think of what could be done to renew their church. The facility became a place of intimacy, informality, and wholeness. The building, the program, and the personnel have proved to be a base for a movement although no plans were made to extend the number of institutes.

The Yokefellow vision took two forms. The first was a residential renewal institute providing a place for the introduction to small groups and the way these groups could renew the church. The second form was the ministries developed by concerned persons to meet discovered needs. Some of these ministries are Industrial Mission, Interfaith Housing for the elderly, Telephone Ministries, Coordinating Clothing and Benevolent Funds of Churches in a local community. Both of these forms were modeled by the first center. The seeds of a movement were being sown; where they sprouted could not be determined in advance. The number of institutes increases whenever a place and people come together and subscribe to the Yokefellow philosophy and symbol.

In December 1958 Robert and Naomi Pickering attended a retreat at the first institute. On May 1, 1959, they organized an ecumenical board under the name Tri-State Yokefellows, near Defiance, Ohio. The Pickerings contributed an old barn and farmland which now has been restored into a unique retreat house. The working together in rebuilding a barn started the renewal of an area. Because of the dedication of the Pickerings they have attracted a variety of persons to their mission. Elton Trueblood led the first retreat. Other persons have been Vartan Melconian, Starr Daily, Thomas Jones, Samuel Emerick, Frank Laubach, Mary Cosby, Thomas Mullen, William Stringfellow, Keith Miller, David Redding, Ger-

trude Behanna, Reuel Howe, Cecil Osborne, Thomas and Amy
Harris. The difference caused by this lay couple in Ohio, Indiana, and Michigan was personalized by the addition of Hope
House in October 1970. In a small home private retreats can
be held over an extended period of time.

Another institute emerged from Midwest Yokefellows origi-
nally based in Chicago. It is named Acorn Yokefellow Center.
The place is sixty miles from Chicago in a woods full of oak
trees. Homer and Alice Dixon purchased the former corporate
lodge for the express purpose of a retreat house. In 1970 Elton
Trueblood, traveling through Chicago, met accidentally at
O'Hare Airport one of the persons who knew of the recent
purchase of the lodge. In their conversation they joined
dreams, Yokefellows and Dixons. James Shaver, a lifelong
friend of Trueblood's and a member of Yokefellows International, was asked to coordinate the relationship. The Acorn
Center was born. Since 1970 Thomas Sampson, Robert Dell,
and John Stahlman were asked to lead the center in the capacity of executive directors. The interesting symbol of this institute in addition to the yoke is Andy Acorn, created by Karen
Thompson. Her husband, Ed Thompson, served as chairman
of the board at the outset. Their interest and zeal combined
with the Dixon generosity and the existing Yokefellows carved
a place for Renewal in a serene place near Chicago, used by
twelve hundred persons the first three years.

A distant place became the next institute. Near Basel,
Switzerland, Hans Schuppli bought a large farm house built in
1796. The Society of Friends helped furnish the house and
provided avenues for the message of the yoke. The "Jochgrup-
pen Haus" (Yokefellow House) opened its doors October 10,
1971. The symbol of the yoke for most Swiss people had a
negative connotation. Schuppli, the inventive director, discovered a positive meaning indigenous to the mountain culture.

From the hills of the village the snow peaks of the Alps can be seen. Two of the highest mountains, Jungfrau and Monk, separated entities of purity, are joined in potential greatness through the "Jungfrau-Joch," the point of juncture between them. This assisted greatly in interpreting the purpose of this new venture.

With the approval of Yokefellows International, the seven Yokefellow disciplines have been reduced to three basic guidelines in Switzerland. First, a daily time of silence, with reading and prayer. Second, obedience through the practice of the Presence. Third, group fellowship and group action in our day-to-day living. A special ministry of this house of the yoke is the stance against all forms of war. The director spent time in prison for his Christian conviction. It also strengthened the movement. Persons from Switzerland, Germany, and Holland, along with visiting Americans, seek inspiration in an exquisitely tranquil place.

An institute with a unique setting is Yokefellows at Shakertown, Kentucky. A historic Shaker village restored to its appearance in the 1850's houses the institute in its West Family Conference Center. Eli Lilly assisted in the restoration and made the invitation possible to Yokefellows. Stephen and Ann Sebert were asked to lead in the creation of another Yokefellow center. They were soon joined by Mary Perdue from Alabama. Similar programs and leadership as developed at Yokefellow Institute in Indiana were held to discern the direction of the center. Soon the center focused on developing groups in the surrounding communities in order to begin the call to the cities to be renewed by Christ. The area of vocational renewal received a welcome response as doctors and bankers came for retreats. The center is now exploring ways to relate more explicitly to the councils of churches. This is being done to plant the call for Renewal more deeply in the heart of the city. The contrasting vision of renewed communities in the midst of an empty Shaker village was not lost on the thirteen hundred participants during the institute's first three years.

Camp Carolwood, near Lenoir, North Carolina, is the location of the retreat center of North Carolina's Yokefellows. Jerry Murray, as a district superintendent of the United Methodist Church, saw the need for the balance in Christianity brought by the yoke. After establishing Yokefellow Cooperative Christian Service Centers in communities, the need arose for retreats to replenish the spiritual wells run dry. A center was built in cooperation with the United Methodist Church of North Carolina and other denominations in 1972. The pattern came from the Carpenter's Lodge of The Dayspring Retreat Center of The Church of the Saviour, Washington, D.C. John Spillman, the director, works closely with the Cooperative Ministries to provide Renewal for those working to renew the communities.

The beginnings of these institutes are better described as centers. A center is a gathering of persons, yet a place where many things are attempted in order to find the immediate need of the region and clarify the specific purpose of the place. This research and development operation provides ample opportunity for interested persons to join. The characteristic of Yokefellows as a research center makes it a renewal agent for the institutional church. If these centers ever begin to see themselves as the church and not as partners with the denominations, Yokefellows will have lost its mission.

Several new starts toward institutes are now in existence. The Yokefellowship of Pennsylvania under the leadership of John Mostoller and the Clarksville, Tennessee, Yokefellow Center with Tony Mavrakos, Director, are the furthest along. The Pennsylvania Center is in relationship to the Christian Church (Disciples of Christ). The Tennessee Center is moving toward establishing intentional communities. This center came from a community church ministering to runaway youth. One of the older international centers ministering to youth without a retreat house is Yokefellows in England. They use St. David's College, Llandudno, North Wales. The movement at the college started with the flowering of many Yokefellow groups of teenage boys but leadership proved hard to maintain in that setting. Lewis and Cato Edwards, not related to each other by family, have been the contact persons for Yokefellows in England. Rev. Cato Edwards and his wife, Hilda, of Epworth, home of the Wesleys, have hosted Yokefellow groups. William Gowland of Luton, England, pioneer in relating the gospel to industry, has spoken at the Yokefellow Conference and led retreats in Yokefellow institutes.

The second basic expression of the yoke is the ministries on the outward journey. Elton Trueblood in 1957 encouraged Cecil Osborne, minister of the First Baptist Church of Burlingame, California, to start Yokefellow groups. Osborne initiated an experimental program for three years. The response to the program by churches and individuals to blending spiritual and psychological disciplines has made possible an international counseling ministry. Most of these Yokefellow groups use psychological tests to help in understanding why they resist the spiritual disciplines. Since 1956 over sixty thousand persons have been in groups started by this center. A staff of ten persons directed by Cecil Osborne and overseen by Mrs. Babette Baker, his competent assistant, enables Osborne to write and travel world wide.

The counseling ministry established similar ministries in Louisiana, California, Alabama, and Texas. Rev. Jim Shelly, Baptist minister, directs the Mid-South Yokefellow Center in Florence, Alabama. Luther Kramer directs The Key in Huntsville, Alabama, and George Hays directs the Gulf-South Yokefellow Center in New Orleans, Louisiana. Another center is Sabbath House located in Dallas, Texas.

The counseling ministry's outreach is to those within Yokefellow groups. By starting the process of sharing the struggle and the joy of personal growth, the "old yoke" is exposed and the "new yoke" of Christ is discovered and fitted with caring persons.

Yokefellowship of Pennsylvania began the second strong ministry of Yokefellows in cooperation with United Churchmen of the Pennsylvania Council of Churches and The New Life Movement of the United Methodist Church. Newman Gaugler and Mickey McConnell have been the key leaders in Pennsylvania. The most significant development has been the prison ministry. The headquarters of The National Prison Ministry is located in Shamokin Dam, Pennsylvania. Although the prison ministry of Yokefellows began in the State of Washington, the major impetus for Yokefellows and prisons has come from Gaugler and McConnell in their travels as laymen in secular work. The objectives of these groups is to provide an experience of belonging to those who feel they belong to no one nor to anything, by means of a fellowship which develops and supports an effort to a Christian way of life in the midst of a cold and alien environment. Over five hundred such groups exist in prisons across America. While developing this national ministry to prisoners the Yokefellows in Pennsylvania gave retreats for prisoners and other seekers. In addition to retreats, a youth center and halfway house have been empowered by this potent fellowship.

A third effective ministry expressing the yoke is North Carolina Yokefellows. There community ministries have been formed ecumenically and the churches in a local community are yoked in common service. The increased effective witness for Christ is no surprise. Yokefellows man telephones, distribute clothing, visit those in prison, serve coffee, and stand ready to respond as a body to the needs of a community. Jerry Murray has pioneered in this combination of ministries and retreats. He saw the vision of the church yoked across cultural and racial lines renewing the city. He enabled others to see and work together by creating the organizational channels for this vision. Now many people and a dozen communities are yoked. Statesville, Lenoir, and Caldwell County are but a few of the communities where a fire was kindled and is burning brighter.

A fourth ministry for the yoke came because Mrs. Tetsuo Kobayashi studied at Earlham College in 1950. Twenty-five years ago the Yokefellow discipline card was printed in Japanese. A person who joins the church pastored by Dr. Tetsuo Kobayashi signs the discipline card. The Christians in Japan work together in one body; therefore they are already yoked. The support from American Yokefellows helped build a kindergarten. The influence of the yoke in Japan has spread to the Republic of China (Taiwan), Thailand, and Malaysia through the linguistic skills of the Kobayashis.

The meditations and vision of Elton Trueblood yoked the hopes and dreams of thousands to renew their hearts, their homes, and their cities. Compared with the millions of persons without this hope, Yokefellow is now just a beginning. Whether it becomes an order that alters the present course of history depends on how many choose to believe it is possible for the church to yoke itself together. The expression of the yoke needed the most is in the cities and towns. These communities are the heart of our society. The question whether it can be done has been answered in North Carolina Yokefellows. The question remains, Will those who call themselves the people of God yoke themselves together to respond to the deep personal and social problems of today? The followers of Christ have done so in the past. As Trueblood understood from reading history, the Benedictine and Franciscan orders were used by God to bring order out of the chaos of the fall of Rome and light to the darkness of the Middle Ages.

We now live in a similar period in history. The Western

civilization crumbles daily before our eyes. The bright lights on the horizon seem nonexistent. But to the discerning eye one ray of light amidst others has been the seed of an order known as Yokefellows. A study of history will show surprising similarities between the founding of orders and the rise of Yokefellows. The need, the seed, the sprouts of three decades are coexistent. The second generation now has the opportunity to water and nurture these beginnings. Some may refuse to hope and others may scoff at such a preposterous goal as all cities renewed, yet the finest flower of the Reformation was the United States of America. The difference between a vision and an illusion is the fruit.